J. P. Hughes

Lyrics of Light

Volume 3

Richardson
DESIGN

Design, layout, typesetting, and cover by Nathan Richardson, nathan@richardsondesign.org; online at richardsondesign.org

Front cover: Lake Louise, Alberta, Canada. Photo taken by the author

© 2011 by J. Preston Hughes
All rights reserved

Any uses of this material beyond those allowed by the exemptions in U.S. copyright law, such as section 107, "Fair Use," and section 108, "Library Copying," require the written permission of the author.

ISBN 978-0-9828085-3-5

*Dedicated to ambassador David M. Kennedy
who taught me to avoid confrontation, treat everybody
the same, and not take the credit*

5/3/12

Sister Harmon
Thank you for
your kind spirit
and efforts in
serving our Lord

AP

Contents

The Gospel

Advice to a Friend 1
Afraid of Dying 3
Spirituality Is Here 4
Brief Shadow 5
Cold Water Baptism 7
The Comforter 8
Compassion 10
Cycles 13
Devotion 14
Dugout 14
Faith 16
The Spirit 20
Go Feed My Sheep 20
First Step 23
Chastise 24
Conversion 25
Courage in Trial 26
Eden 28
Emotion 31

Faith Precedes the Miracle 31
Favorite Phrase 34
Fellowship 35
Gently Lift 36
Ghana 38
Gifts 42
Handcart 44
Holy Ghost 47
Ice to Thaw 49
Jeremiah 52

THOUGHTS ON LIFE

Almost Homeless 55
The Voices 58
The Demand 60
I Am New 61
Duty Trumps Desire 61
Observations 62
Changing Times 64
Avoided 65
Advertising 65
Earwiggian 66
Exchange 67
Exploration 69
Go and Report 69
Knowing 72

Life's Motion 72
Life of Time 73
Bold 76
Coincidence 77
Harv 78
Seeker 78
Build a Tradition 83
Buyer Seller 85
Can't Sleep 88
Debris 89
Desire 90
Distraction 92

Memories and Events

My School Eye Exam 95
Biking Back 96
I Was Lost 98
Convert 98
Exchange 99
Cabin Hammock 101
Ingestion 104
Flying above the Clouds 106
Silence Sweet 107
Christmas Program 115
Bishop's History 117
Easy Money 120

A Midsummer Night's Dream. 121
Testimonies. 123
Russian Class. 125
LDS General Conference 133
Funeral of E. R. McKay 137
Galapagos 148
Sacrament Meeting 150
Temple Session. 158
Sacrament Meeting Mother's Day. 162
Ray Liddell. 170
Mickey Hansen. 171
Carmen. 173
Carol Lee. 175
Mike 177
Four Years Old. 177
Ghana Child 177
Harp Music. 180
La Bohème. 181
Priesthood Executive Meeting 181
"Last Man Out" 183

Community and Politics

Leed 191
Rotary 194
Republican Precinct Chair Meeting. 198
Pornography Leadership. 208

Salt Lake Community College 214
Rotary and the Tax. 225
President Monson 228
Hinckley Institute 236
To Fold Clothes 241
Bully 244
Health Care Reform 247
Our Experiment 250

Medicine

A Letter 253
Innovation 254
Ovarian Cancer 259
Cancer 261
Stay Here. 262
Salt Lake Surgical 263
American Cancer Society 270
IMC Surgery Department 277
Decisions. 279
Foreign Bodies. 280
ACLS. 282
Addiction. 286
Health Department Grant. 286

The Gospel

Advice to a Friend

Advice to Bishop Essig
Will be small, not big
To remember this knight
And evil around to fight

It is a celebration
His calling an illustration
It is hard to give advice
My experience to splice

It is a challenging role
The price has a high toll
There are lessons to learn
Mainly to spiritually discern

Lyrics of Light

The inspiration of the call
And our time to stand tall
This work is for another
Time and effort to cover

The counselors of power
Three enlightened empower
This is the work of God
The one we praise and laud

It is a time you should ask
"Why not" complete the task
Your system will be fine
Names and problems remind

An attitude to be kind
But must spend the time
There is no preparation
Other than revelation

Each life is the difference
The spiritual is the reference
Love your clerks
Respect their works

Appreciate those who try
Be soft when they cry
Keep deep things close within
Discussing about another's sin

The enlightened one
For diversity to come
Should have a smile
Keep it on for a while

Make a visit or call
Contacting one and all
Delegate the power
Not demanding or sour

Let the calling flow
Where the Lord will show
Ask him, "Is there yet more?"
And you will see an open door

Afraid of Dying

I would be lying
If not afraid of dying
Life here complying
My belief not denying
The physical not complying

Things of the past
I thought would last
Playing my part in the cast
Of where I was placed to bask

Lyrics of Light

When everything is in pain
Then why do we remain?
Life does not remain the same
Nor will I always be sane

So each day will contain
Energy and wisdom remain
Leaving will not detain
The soul of our domain

When nothing works
And dementia lurks
It might be best
To finish the test

When we put down the pen
Then will our heart depend
No longer to just contend
On the next phase to send

Spirituality Is Here

Spirit is here
Rejoicing near
Edwin family effect
Memories reflect

Be an example
Gospel to sample

Lord knows beginning
And release from sinning

Live with God forever
Ties to earth sever
Lord knows all
For us to call

Baptism after faith
Listened what saith?
Not last step
Life to prep

Promise to help you
Power alone with few
Sacrament to feel
Baptism we seal

Little steps to go
Along Christ's show
How will we know?
Spirituality will flow.

Brief Shadow

Brief shadow
Grief to show
Only a moment
Message content

Birth life new
Resurrection clue
Message to live
Message to give

"Savior of the World"
In the play unfurled
Angel on the inside
Standing there beside

On the rolling stone
Shadow cross was shown
We can believe
With sight conceive

We can know
From hands to show
In our unbelief
We know with relief

It was so subtle and fast
It did not last when passed
A shadow on a round rock
Of the door we all knock

"And it shall be opened"
"And it shall be opened"

It may be from our own hands to see
It may be our hands seen by Thee
That He can know
What our hands show

So that he can believe
What of us to conceive
That he may know
That He may know

What to believe
Faith in us relieve
So that we open the door
In our Resurrection adore

This our spiritual creator
This our impression's mentor
So that we can say
Our door is open today

Cold Water Baptism

Thoughts at the baptismal service of Jimmy Newman. There was no hot water, but Jimmy entered the font without complaint.

Cold water and cough
Still the feeling soft
Baptism of Jimmy Newman
Who is now a new man

Humble my guide
The Spirit supplied
Standing as so many
With love of all and any

Who in discomfort
To the Lord report
I will do what it takes
To change what it makes

From this discomfort
In silence I report
This was a great day
This is a memory to stay

The Comforter

The third member
We should remember
Is the Holy Ghost
Of our Spirit to host

Holy in Latin "ho-li"
Means "whole" we see
It also means "well"
Or complete to tell

Ghost is "gost" or "gast"
In Latin language to last

This descriptive word now
Is "seat of life" somehow

This is the foundation
Of intelligence's inspiration
The Holy Ghost is the Spirit
For all in life who hear it

The name of Comforter
Is the power for sure
"Com" means together
With us in any weather

"Fortor" means strong
"Fortis" all along
To impart strength
For any tested length

For hope in prayer
Each and all aware
The "whole" of all
Is our deepest call

The Holy Spirit
Is where we fit
With the "breath" of soul
The Spirit of life to roll

The strength for us all
Is the Spirit's highest call
Ghost means "breath" demand
And "He breathed in to man"

"The breath of life" to know
To live and to show
That we now understand
That we live His command

Compassion

Inspired by a talk given by Garry Mitchell

"What manner are ye?"
Am I as Thee?
Gentile and kind
Healing the blind

Martha and Mary
Disciple sick to carry
Paintings that trace
The Lord's face and place

Reach out and touch
Helping one on a crutch
Pioneers came in poverty
Comfort, was sharing charity

Service is selfless
His example to redress
Agent of the Lord
A calling to afford

Mercy in weakness
Strength with meekness
Baptismal covenant
His Spirit dependent

"He will be with us"
Helping in life's fuss
Love them all
Distractions fall

Hands come down
When helping around
"Friends like pillars"
Standing, holding thrillers

Leaning or just there
Friendship now aware
Changes when we care
Seeing when we stare

Reach
Teach
Teach
Reach

Put arm around
Voice with a sound
Friend now found
Joined now bound

Stranger taken in
Understanding will begin
"Done to the least of these"
Done unto me in ease

My son was born deaf
Now patience left
Apprentice to change
Training to arrange

He heard the birds
He heard the words
Shelling fresh peas
Christmas to appease

Father and son come home
Visiting and helping roam
Put your arm around
Then you hear the sound

Cycles

Inspired by a talk given by Larry Jameson

> Those who are righteous
> Kind, soft, humble to light us
> Agency to be free
> Choices to agree
>
> Prosperity when we try
> Science, progress to apply
> Improvement not to deny
> Energy work and industry
>
> Comfort in choices
> Seeking different voices
> Morality in decline
> Greed is just fine
>
> Pride will collide
> Wickedness imbibe
> Collapse perhaps
> Relapse synapse
>
> Then we want a change
> To righteousness arrange
> Start with the basics
> Avoiding what afflicts

The cycles begins again
The timeline only when
We feel deeper inside
With our soul confide

Devotion

Inspired by a talk given by Marin Copeland

What is the commotion?
About our devotion
When we promise and care
Tithing is a way to share

Dugout

The pioneer dugout
What is that about?
Dig a hole in the ground
That is where you are found

Protection from the weather
No choices of whether
We want to live
Our life to give

Walking across the plains
Many dying with pains

J. P. Hughes

Nothing when they got here
Poverty suffering so near

Dig a hole in the hill
Cover the opening from the chill
Dirt floor and small window
Looking out at the blowing snow

It was cold
For huddling bold
It was a struggle
The family had to snuggle

My family left this place
To live in a different space
I found a small history
Of the 1800s mystery

And my great-grandfather
Who made mah-lasses as a farmer
Moved and built a new adobe home
For four generations to roam

His son was a teacher
After a mission as a preacher
Who became a physician
Living, working within

His son, my father and me
Were born and lived to see
From very humble beginning
A dugout from the digging

Was four generations of return
From gratitude we discern
The decision is my concern
From their sacrifice we earn

The willingness to dig in
For protection to begin
Then move to build
Our families to shield

But more to pay back
From our life intact

"Here am I"
From Thy command
For any demand
Sacrifice and remand

Faith

Inspired by a talk given by David Allart

Looking toward
Faith in the Lord

What is it?
Belief to fit

"Things hoped for"
Unseen and more
"Things that are true"
Actions, power in you

Decision's out of blue
Life direction's to construe
"Faith is work"
Belief not to shirk

You may acquire
Information aspire
Knowledge and fire
If we will inquire

Parsing words and belief
With faith within relief
Contrasts "in good faith"
History visual, as it saith

Knowledge without seeing
Understand in our being
Certainty Israel is there
Old history to be aware

I know people where
Study, learn wisdom, care
Plant to harvest and glean
Hope and invest in the unseen

Principle of endorsement
Faith with contentment
I have studied and know
Knowledge, faith to show

If a fact is accepted
Faith and knowledge is reflected
No longer just believe
Or a testimony conceive

Spirit bears a witness
Full of hope to address
The voice of the Spirit
When quietly, we hear it

Leading by emotion
Understanding devotion
How do you judge?
Spirit or emotion budge

Doubt or to question?
Or answer a spiritual suggestion
Witness to identify
Soberness make you cry

Revelation of another
Valid for the will to cover
Listening to doubt
Responsibly about

"Have to be there"
Your choice to care
Doubt is in the stare
Distraction is the snare

Diversions are not fair
Deafens with the blare
"Why" in the question
"Perfect" is the suggestion

Act in the Lord's name
Your efforts the same
Receive strength to avoid
Temptations from the void

If we can believe
Then obey not deceive
We may fall short
Faith lost or abort

"Believe doubting nothing"
Then for first time seeing
We gave it a merciful try
Faith is what we should apply

The Spirit

> The Spirit is my friend
> My counselor to the end
> Instruction to blend
> Judgment to mend
>
> Knowledge to send
> Understanding to attend
> My testimony to defend
> Doubts to contend

Go Feed My Sheep

> "Feed my sheep
> Feed my sheep
> Feed my sheep"
> Repeated three to keep
>
> I Am the bread of life
> To feed those with strife
> This is from Me
> Spiritual blessings be
>
> "Take this bread" and eat
> In remembrance of My feet
> Visit those who are blind
> "For they are mine"

J. P. Hughes

"Feed My sheep"
It will make you weep
"My promise I will keep
Spiritually with my sheep"

We can all serve the Lord
Bonded with one accord
Taught in the same place
Service with a Christian face

What is the coincidence
In an assignment's incidence
Of young and old
Experience shared and told

You are part of His fold
You are warm and not cold
Visit the elderly and infirm
Then to you I will confirm

How can we learn?
Of another's concern
Walking up those stairs
Like our Father cares

"You are the Dad" I never had
It made me very sad
"Feed My sheep"
It will make you weep

My promise I will keep
Spiritually with My sheep
Now in the Master's promise new
You will understand and renew

"Thank you for the bread"
As we left she said
This was not just for me
A spiritual blessing to see

"I Am the bread of life"
Take a loaf to the widower's wife
Your joy will be
When you "do it for Me"

I needed this
Not to be remiss
"Hard to be a pianist blind"
In a church same as mine

Listen to the talking
Could get there walking
Experience could make you cry
Tonight answers when we try

"Go feed My sheep"
It will make you weep

First Step

Inspired by a lesson given by Chuck Cole

"Watch the first step"
Unwelcome it crept
Replaced a thought
For faith we sought

Remember mother
Child or brother
"Invitation only"
Thought is lonely

Cultivate change
Temple arrange
Pray for strength
Christ-centered length

Let go of addictions
With parasitic inflictions
Why do we choose?
When we will lose

Serve those in need
Enough I plead
Set priorities
For tears to ease

The respect and love
Sanctity from above
Temptation has no place
"Enemy of my soul" and face

Move away from disgrace
Controlling my taste
In my mind's space
Leave what will debase

Chastise

Inspired by Mike Barnhurst

Chastise
Made wise
Contention
Retention

Question
Suggestion
Lord we knew
Sweet unto to you

Lord said no
Our parable show
I am honest
I am not the best

He exalted the abased
Love all "I embraced"
"You are blessed"
When you confessed

Conversion

Inspired by Dan Stevens

My own conversion
With spiritual emersion
Comes from principles
Direction of the disciples

I had curiosity to know
From Tennessee to show
I believed in tithing
This fundamental ring

The contribution of being
With the Spirit to sing
Basic ideas to inspire
Holy Ghost in heart and fire

"I had seen" to redeem
Times were not so clean
"Do not mess with it"
Obedience through the Spirit

Give others a chance
In the Messiah's dance
Struggle to befriend
Obey until the end

It all starts with a change of heart
"Anti-regression medication" to impart
Recommit to prayer
Stay converted and aware

Courage in Trial

Inspired by Liesli Shurtliff

Take courage in a trial
Offer your prayers awhile
Ask is it true?
The soft whisper is a clue

Answers since time
Began to rhyme
Promise and the wall
Prayer written for all

Receive after a knock
Our rejections to block
A prayer for health
Knowledge or wealth

Answers in a fashion
Definitive in compassion
Not just wishing
Nor spiritual fishing

Effective gift
Peace to lift
Not a dividing fence
Comforting suspense

It is simple and quick
"In mind and heart" so slick
Need listening skills
Deep quieting chills

Answers are clear
No super thought fear
In scriptures is the word
Where answers occurred

More questions annoy
Frustration's toy
Reason to build
Instrument to yield

Faith and love to solve
Disconnect to resolve
Saved by grace
Faith, work, and space

Do all we can
Exercise a capacity plan
Walk on your own
Lord's logic condone

Humility is not blurred
In scripture occurred
Asking not for the contrary
But just a sincere inquiry

It is a means to learn
His will and concern
Ask questions to be right
In this life's competing fight

Eden

Sister Eden Dall
Rome Italy call
To serve a mission
To receive His commission

To this sacred place
A city to embrace
The history of our Savior
In art's mosaic to savor

Teaching to change behavior
To the spiritual craver

The law and His glory
Is the center of this story

"Be Still My Soul"
Is the Spirit's goal
Sacred to arise and shout
Temple dedication about

Joyful enthusiasm
Winter Quarter's chiasm
Now I look back
No courage to lack

Of peace of thought
Weekly I sought
Covenant learning
Obedience yearning

All leads to a temple place
That you will find a space
To bring memory to the dead
All joined restored as He said

Obedient to build
Salvation to yield
Preparation
Foundation

Symbolic meaning
Preparation seaming
Ponder before
Prayer at the door

Looked to the day
To visit and pray
No sacrifice too great
Family endowed to contemplate

Love across the veil
Protection to avail
True joy and happiness
Commanded no guess

More than stone
Attending not alone
They are a beacon
Foundation not of sand

Unites and welds us to Thee
"It means a lot to me"
"I know it is true"
It can be the same for you

"I have seen it in my life"

Emotion

> The transfer of emotion
> The art is this devotion
> Will avoid commotion
> And our confrontation

Faith Precedes the Miracle

> Faith precedes the willing to serve
> Another's soul you may conserve
> It is never what you will expect
> When of this time you reflect
>
> It is the sensitivity of the listening
> It is the impression glistening
> It is our just being there
> With expression of care
>
> It is seeing the work
> Witness and not shirk
>
> The miracle is in the order
> The miracle is in the sacrifice
> The miracle is in the visit
> The miracle is in the detail
> The miracle is in the effort
> The miracle is in the soft
> The miracle is in the quiet

The miracle is in the small

"Faith precedes the miracle"
Like an inner nerve may tickle
I am willing to love
This decision about above

Has already been made
With light, shadow, and shade
Miracle is defined
With meaning refined

In Russian "Mir" means
Village, it now seems
In Latin it means "miraculum"
Held tight as a tenaculum

Or a word part "mirari"
"To wonder" then to see
It is a deviating event
From our nature content

It transcends our knowledge
Superhuman on a ledge
But "natural to the divine"
Learned where we are refined

Faith is that "which is believed"
Faith is that which is conceived

Latin word "feid" *fei* in "fidelity
Means trust, duty and loyalty

Our belief with confidence
Will make the difference
Precede is Latin "pracedere"
Or "prae" as in just before

But the key to me
Was to agree
The meaning of "ceder"
Is the message greeter

"To go" before to see
"To go" in front with Thee
"To go" in order of time
"To go" in life and mind

Ask yourself where was I?
Ponder the time of this miracle to cry?
Who are you with at the moment?
This is the time to comment

Do not put the miracle down
In sarcasms to drown

"Well that was a miracle"

It is coincidence or "Divine Design"
It is the connections of all to remind

"Faith precedes the miracle"

Favorite Phrase

I have a favorite phrase
It will and still amaze
"This is as good as it gets"
Cool, soft, silence, peace, no regrets

I have an inner voice
Talking almost without my choice
Many times by coincidence
I or it speaks with insistence

Saying "There is a God"
Proving "There is a God"
Observing "There is a God"
Smiling "There is a God"

I have a wife very dear
My happiness when near
E. J. said this morning
With voice cordoning

"I am having a breakdown"
While she was looking around
I told her that she was not
Our peaceful home clean without a spot

"You are not having a breakdown"
You are just breaking down
With my humor and as a clown
I can bring her a smile not a frown

Fellowship

Inspired by Randy Keller

Tender mercy in fellowship
Kindness in our friendship
I felt the Spirit
To be close and near it

Listen with devotion
It is natural emotion
Pride is the gateway
All else will say

Church is true
Guidance for you
Humble your self
Or be on Lord's shelf

There is a deeper place
With our sober face
Scroll is known
Duty to assist shown

Lyrics of Light

    Share the light
    Blessings bright
    Answers sought
    Advise is taught

    From the Book
    Study, take a look
    It is word of God
    The one we applaud

    "Some have been offended"
    Lightened burdens defended
    Include others
    Our lost brothers

Gently Lift

Inspired by Larry Lawrence

    Angel of John
    Placed hand belong
    Think of joy
    Surprise employee

    Aaronic Priesthood
    Conferred understood
    Lesser of keys
    Outward to please

Agent to carry
Administration bury
Holy Ghost to heed
Knowledge need

Power plead
Joy concede
Peace in deed
From inner need

Ministering cup
Gently lift to sup
Tender wept
Joy kept

Morally clean
Spiritually lean
"Give me a young man"
Performing a miracle can

Individual qualify
Counsel apply
Obligation and blessing
Magnify and dressing

Live worthy now
Blessed to endow
Lord needs you
Declared to few

Parents of teens
Answers steams
Impression seems
Insight gleams

Not easy be strong
Try to get along
Courageous parent
In danger if content

Ghana

There is a green field
Ghana Saints to yield
It is so touching
Beauty of song reaching

Small children singing
The deep Spirit bringing
"Oh God, thee Eternal Father"
Passing sacrament by a brother

It is the Ola Ward to apply
With a white shirt and tie
Humming hot with fans
Red-tiled roof commands

Thirty-two in the choir
The congregation to inspire

Soloist and with the organ
Smiling pleading when began

Youth speaker reading
Better life with God conceding
"Meet with Jesus" a voice
The decision is your choice

"I know what said is true"
Loving Father's life ensue
Heavenly Father will hear
We promised to be near

We forget Him sometimes
"How close are we" to find
"Meditate and contemplate"
The meaning to substantiate

Prayer is the yearning"
Loyalty then learning
Humility is a virtue
A theme is from you

God will inspire
No money to require
Sick hunger to resolve
Not own Savior to solve

"I say all this"
Name of Jesus not miss
Young woman to talk
How to walk the walk

On this coastal shore
Of wealth and humanity adore
Black with a heart sincere
"Asking for the gospel" to appear

Opportunity to learn
With speaking concern
Search a child's eyes
Walking, looking tries

To see this white guy
It could make you cry
Song numbers clock on wall
Speaker with passion standing tall

Voice is a foreign language
Asking for the Spirit to assuage
"Answers are in our prayer"
To make us more aware

"Live the answer"
In your lives of care
For Jesus Christ's love
He cares from above

People with dignity
Honesty and integrity
Gathered from the palm
Volcanic surf and balm

Selected from red sand
Thatched rock and rattan
It is "amazing grace"
To look into their face

Tiled floors so clean
Smiles that just beam
Color on cloth batik
Sitting with the Lord to seek

Look around where we are
Full moon and lonely star
Each window decorated with a bar
"Trust the Lord" so far

Sitting with reverence
Obedience is the reference
Here working with you
Speaking "I know it is true"

The idea is that we all need to float
All together in God's hand carved boat
The ending song "Do what is right"
"Let consequences follow" in sight

"Truth reflects on our senses" ever more
Singing "reach that blissful shore"
"Angels wait to join us"
Next life without this fuss

Gifts

Inspired by Mason Haywood

Gift of the Spirit
How to get near it
Faith as a gift
Need to use to lift

Prompted to do
Discovery for you
Tongues as a gift
Communication's drift

Situations and space
Discerning pace
The future to ask
A gift of the task

Cannot name all
Depends on your call
Life and situation
Gift of translation

Virtuous and clean
Warning's lean
Learning not know
Interpretation condone

Spoken with understanding
"What's going on" demanding
Gifts to discern
In deception's burn

Given to know
Our belief to show
"Gift of administration"
Gift of diversity of operation

Gift of wisdom
Gift of word for some
Gift of faith to be healed
Gift of some to heal

Gift of miracles preform
Given in time of storm
"Ask in Spirit
Receive in Spirit"

That is "the will of God"
Subtle as a slight nod
Blessed with ability
Knowledge's stability

Put into a situation
Pressure of the condition
It will be a knock on a door
The gift will enter and reassure

Handcart

1856 handcart travel
The feelings unravel
Left too late
Traveling fate

No food
Surely mood
Early winter cold
Testing the bold

It was the time
With God in mind
Metaphor to commit
Pulling by hand bit by bit

Five hundred strong
Few felt it was wrong
With miracles along the way
Praying for a better day

Seeing people who did not stay
With death and burial to pay

There were wolves and snakes
Flower meal Dutch oven bakes

How can I write?
Of their fear and flight
I never have had starvation
Nor pulled with exhaustion

Never alone nor poor
Never fleeing to endure
I know the story
Even parts gory

I know of God
The One we applaud
I know the cost
I know the lost

I have been on the trail
I know the tale
I have been to every place
I have seen the open space

What was left behind?
Their sacrifice to remind
The burial of the children
Wife, husband and friend

There is no way to compare
This story we share
It makes me cry
Even question why

It came from belief
The effort of relief
Keeping the story alive
By those who did survive

Who became the settlers?
Farmers, miners, and tellers
"I was there"
"I saw" everywhere

The hand of demand
The sacrifice by command
We are all travelers now
Different times somehow

To love our wife and family
Love of the children we see
Love of this Heavenly Spirit
And the importance of being near it

Holy Ghost

Inspired by Janie Kauffman

Holy Ghost as a gift
Purifies our soul to lift
Constant Companion
Friend with impression

To guide in light
To learn beside sight
To enjoy creation
To receive inspiration

Bearing witness to truth
Obedience as of Ruth
Enlightened and faithful
Desires most fruitful

All conscience splice
In this Light of Christ
All will be good
Inspired as could

Another source
Uniformly of course
Everywhere and equal
Mercy in the sequel

Lyrics of Light

Terminology of light
Guardian angel delight
Blessing and obligation
Follow the suggestion

Comes as a good idea in time
Logical practical of my mind
But then I did not listen
Still thinking to glisten

Truth will confirm
True in word, feeling learn
Comforted then you know
"It is all right" to go

See I will show it true
"I will not leave you"
Comfortless or blue
The direction is new

"Life's going well"
Healing you to tell
Now you can discern
Of your life and concern

Ice to Thaw

Inspired by the apostle David A. Bednar

Need to strive
With our lives
Religions of the day
Baptism what to say

The Comforter teacher
Revelator and preacher
Witness of the Son
Testimony begun

Power convincing
Redeemer not mincing
Baptism of Fire
Following desire

"We heard"
Voice not blurred
Baptism by emersion
Not Son in diversion

Channel to see
Principle and me
Confirm is simple
Profound dimple

"Receive the Holy Ghost"
Significance of this Host
Not a passive act
Action was fact

Desire to live
This gift to give
Giver of the gift
Companion will lift

Sincere desire
Invite require
Obey is empire
Never to retire

Pray in earnest
Distraction's test
Invitation required
Sincerity desired

Cannot command
Cannot demand
Covenant and pray
Search scriptures today

Seek and lift thought
Study action sought
Do not withdraw
Ice to thaw

Listen to sacrament prayer
Remember be aware
Do and become
Reasons of some

Retain light
Knowledge bright
Reasons to reflect
Temple kindred respect

Gather in unity
Obeying duty
Over the quest
Review the best

Companion receive
Strive to conceive
Exactness to keep
Command to leap

True by the way
Truth light today
Receive the Holy Ghost
Do not fall nor boast

Humble and faithful
Deliberate and careful
Keep still voice
Going choice

Lyrics of Light

Heart open and soft
Voices in the loft
Joy to the soul
Is a pleasant goal

Be good
Build as should
"They will go right"
The future is bright

The ultimate teacher
For the believing creature
Is the Holy Spirit
Live to be near it

Jeremiah

Inspired by Cindy and Don Butterfield

He was beaten in prison
But an iron pillar decision
He was foreordained
The council contained

'I know thee"
Your life to see
"I sanctified thee"
"I ordained thee"

J. P. Hughes

For what you would be
You have been called by Me
"I will speak for you"
Knowledge will flow true

Fear not their face
From your deeper space
"I will put in the word"
Your mission not absurd

The call extended
The time amended
Living on the edge
Closest to the ledge

"I see a rod"
After question from God
"What seest thou ?
A seething pot now

I see a gate and wall
That will break and fall
Touching wickedness
With hands and dress

Mend your way
Now obey
Words in ears
Warning nears

Hearth with fire
Hidden to inspire
Write the word
After feeling occurred

Sent to tell
Repentance swell
What to learn
Of life's concern

Broken cistern
No water discern
Forsaken water of me
Now distracted from Thee

Turn from the fountain
Rely on me to retain
Your ways will correct
After bitterness detect

We are a mold
Obey when told

Thoughts on Life

Almost Homeless

A young man in my ward whom I spent a lot of time with in the bishop's office

> I would be without a home
> This cold city to roam
> I have a place to stay
> Even though I cannot pay
>
> I just got out of jail
> My past life did fail
> My choices to sell drugs
> Spent locked up with thugs

He did not have a job
I asked him to see Bob
He did not know
Just where to go

He did not have a map
No one to give a crap
He had no car
Would not walk far

He smoked a chain
Bad habits remain
He was good to enable
A gift of others a fable

His requests to urge
Last time a surge
Hard to follow up
His habits corrupt

No driver license
No common sense
No education dent
Home from mission sent

Will not do little things
Obligation that brings
Good to blame
Circumstance the same

Not paying his way
Roommate did convey
Seeing old friends
When this story ends

Young man who also came
Patterns and habits the same
He was homeless
No way to help or confess

He was a friend in jail
Had habits persist to tell
Saw LDS Family Services
Mental health to preserve us

Needing medication
Depressive suicide direction
Did not know who to call
Had a name, that was all

"Will you help me some way?"
Doctors, medication, food, rent to pay
This problem is complex
The source creation's index

A young life
Filled with strife
Here to just get by
Will not give it a try

Lied on all applications
Jail, drugs, and supplications
"No one to give advice"
Would not take it concise

A better life to splice
A deep meaning suffice
Leave manipulation's device
Of life the roll of the dice

I may confide
He will time divide
Where to reside
Me at his side

Hard to help the one
Whose life is no fun?
Outcome and trial soon done
Life's responsibility to run

The Voices

Listening to the voices
Changing my choices
Where do they come?"
Fleeting most with some

When to react?
Where do I act?

J. P. Hughes

How do you know?
A memory to show

How do you train?
A mind to remain
Living in the present
What is my intent?

What is the plan?
To do what I can
Where are the voices?
When making choices

Is it all about feeling?
What is the sealing?
You can change
Lives rearrange

Avoiding the things
That sorrow brings
Do not get in
What might be sin?

Does it feel good?
Doing what we should

The Demand

Filling the demand
Following the command
Finding the open hand
Finalizing the remand

Do what is asked
Help complete the task
Discover one to bask
Return the gift that lasts

Responsively kind
Respecting the mind
Repairing the find
Reporting on time

We need permission
For our commission
To be in submission
Completing remission

Listen
Action
Observation
Completion

I Am New

    Today I am new
    And from Kenya, too
    I am here to meet with you
    Tell me what to do

    Where should I go?
    To learn and earnestly know
    What is above and there below?
    That would answer as winds blow

    A sound through the door
    Dare I ask anymore?
    New life and answer sure
    From wind raging roar

    You will receive
    You will believe
    Your heart relieve
    Now life achieve

Duty Trumps Desire

    Duty trumps my desire
    More relaxed I aspire
    A deeper breath respire
    Then time enough retire

I put off what I want to
So duty can require all I do
The inner peace with you
Must be my creation too

Not spending all my time
Humming someone else's rhyme
But as the life clocks chime
I take care of the soul that is mine

Observations

Observations
Contemplations
Reflections
Deflections

They do not know
How they show
What is missing?
From just kissing

Marriage sealing
Life revealing
Relationship dealing
Maturity appealing

To commit
To submit

To remit
To admit

This is a better way
Is what I can say
Old with young
Not far flung

Smiles of hope
Clean as soap
They will not miss
What about this?

All are in a state
Living their fate
It is not too late
To contemplate

They shall walk and be
Their stand with Thee
If they agree
Covenant with Me

If they break
Their promise take
Then as a fake
Their life forsake

They lose the power
This very hour
Their actions sour
And sadness devour

Have no sexual relation
Commitment's ablation
Until marriage time
Creation sublime

The physical stage
A time engage
Emotions enrage
Turning life's page

Deepening impart
Love from the heart
The spiritual part
With a purity start

Changing Times

Moral drift
Never lift
Life to linger
Temporal finger

Visited by fire
Changes most dire

Living in recess
Of this process

Charity tomorrow
Change life's sorrow
Deep bone marrow
Little time to borrow

Avoided

Avoid out of respect
Not friendly aspect
Never get to know
Who never show?

Any nod of greeting
At any meeting
Not because we like
In common spite

Advertising

TV advertising a pet "peticure" ad
Floor cleaning ad also sad
Media advertising so glad
It is as awful as it is so bad.

Earwiggian

There is nothing more viable
And continuation more survivable
Than a crawling small
Earwig scurrying among all

Stuff that is on the ground
Stuff that is spread around
You can not kill
Nor smash or instill

Any kind of life ending
With all your force sending
You can step on it
You can crush and spit

It will just move along
When you have gone
People are just like that
For observations, I sat

They can smoke and take drugs
Follow violence like thugs
They can be arrested
From what is attested

They just bounce back
From good judgment's lack

Yet they live forever
In survival's endeavor

You have to hand it to them
By the time their life will end

Exchange

The emphasis is who
   Takes
The essence is who
   Gives
The receiver takes
   Time
Of clothing and toys to
   Find
The giver comes and
   Goes
Slight and quick as the wind
   Blows
Who can ever judge
   Another
In poverty that will
   Smother
One brings in a new
   Sack
Others come to find what they
   Lack

Lyrics of Light

Infant's dark happy eyes
   Move
Looking along a searching
   Groove
Looking for milk bottle to
   Suck
Being here with Mom for
   Luck
Those who take in for
   Need
Now service and help
   Plead
Giver now the helping
   Poor
Smiling, taking, sorting
   More
Small ones and
   Old
Coming in from the
   Cold
Some here just to
   Return
Others working with
   Concern
Every language
   Spoken
Donations but now a

Token
Life that is not totally
    Complete
The Creator loves all
    Repeat

Exploration

Anonymous; heard on TV

We shall not cease
From exploration

At the end of our
Exploring

We will arrive where
We started

And know the place
For the first time

Go and Report

Go and return
Confidence to earn
In diversity we are one
Knowing when it is done

It may be a call
To many or to all
It may be a personal voice
Obeying is our choice

To hear then do
Is important for you
To return and report
Consolidation to import

It completes the circuit
Then assumptions not intuit
No longer just assume
But with progress resume

Then confidence is strong
As we all move along
In the computer world
Receive and send unfurled

In the military an order
To protect that border
In medicine one is told
In surgery order is bold

In religion we obey
The changes to convey
In education we teach
Then testing to reach

It is the question
Then answer's suggestion
In the synapse of a nerve
The connection deserve

Everything can be solved
If the follow up is resolved
It is more than "go and do"
It is the report from me to you

Then we know that it is done
Life takes on more fun
It is the joy of accomplishment
Not the unsettled wonderment

It is a law of hearing
It is a joy of endearing
It is one working today
It is more than just play

It is the system complete
Knowing and done replete
Then the next to build
Then the next to shield

Go and return
More than concern
Go and return
The principle to learn

Knowing

People who don't know criticize
People who do know eulogize
People who think they know synthesize
People who doubt what they know compromise
People who do not doubt what they know cannot empathize
People who delay what they know agonize
People who do not see what they know generalize
People who hate what they know compartmentalize

Life's Motion

It is the motion
Of life's commotion
The tests of devotion
During the promotion

Life is dedication
Not just flotation
Not for adulation
Not sensory ablation

Life is the change
Time to rearrange
Not just to derange
Nor act very strange

The motion of it all
Atoms and electrons fall
Color and heat install
Our eyes to enthrall

Motion is the child
Acting and running wild
Motion is the old
Doing what is told

We always will move
In or out of the groove
It is the destiny of all
To stand up tall

Life of Time

Life in harmony's time
Music strings in rhyme
The efforts to set it up
Repetitive not corrupt

Never got to play
The music today
The song unsung
From where unstrung

It is from our desire
What plays from the wire

What is tense and in tune
Our passion reflected moon

If an unlatched door
Or a foreign shore
We played and won
In the sun and fun

Sounds of beauty high
Listening makes you cry
Celtic strings apply
Feelings never deny

Dance of flight
In the dawn's light
Promises where we row
Waves move and flow

Spin, skip, and step
Our lyrical dance kept
Jump, lean, bow, and lift
Music of rhythm's gift

Who knows when you believe
This time of life conceive
You cannot explain
Nor understand if sane

It is the miracle to believe
This time of life relieve
The stars in the back
The moment we may lack

Are the times we say
It is now time to pray
The drums will beat
The intensity neat

The people will meet
The music to repeat
Let me stay
Not sail away

Just for a day
Meaning convey
The leaf of color left
Falling from time's cleft

Is the true
Is the you
Is what is left behind
That continues to remind

What we are
From so far
Part of a star
Judged at the bar

Bold

You do not have to be bold
To do what you are told
Just stand out in the cold
And get to know the fold

Moses's plea, "Let my people go"
The Lord's power to show
LDS modern cry to the door of tin
Please just let my people in.

I walked across the street
Samoan people to meet
Standing at the door four
Line in back for many more

They were here at six
I joined them to fix
A plan to get inside
And with Lord abide

People without tickets pass where
I told them about line on Temple Square
Freezing together outside
In a warm seat will confide

Coincidence

Standing in the front outside
Was this man where I reside?
With his two sons and twin brother
Just visiting with another

It added to the reason
Of this spiritual season
Why go with the Spirit flow
God can touch deep to know

PGH helped his son's mission
Ben in Brazil for submission
Conner standing there as well
With a brother Jesse to tell

Two brother, two brother, too
Father and son with uncle true
Missionaries first from Oshkosh,
Wisconsin, but north a bit, my gosh

Singing to troops of street
Drown out tormentors to beat
Surprise birthday dinner
With roommate a winner

Harv

    Write without thinking
    Leave without planning
    Relationships without commitment
    Nature is bloody thing
    Red in tooth and claw

Seeker

Inspired by a talk by Dee Darling

    We need to be curious
    About the impervious
    Seeker after the truth
    Not found in any booth

    We need to go and be
    A seeker of the beauty
    A place where we can see
    A museum of life from Thee

    We need to have integrity now
    Just say what we mean and how
    Speak what we know is the right
    Stay honest in our mind's sight

    Compassion is a must
    Charity for all is just

Treating people the same
So that our heart will remain

This is religious liturgy
When learned in surgery
Cut is to cure
Ligate for sure

Idea taught from Dee
Given in light to me
Unpeeled as an onion
From Lowell Bennion

This spiritual thought
Happiness we sought
Disillusion we fight
No happiness in sight

No happiness hangs on another
No hand of praise from a brother
Power is in the saying
Hard life is the paying

Joyful in control
You pay the toll
Help with the sick
In the business flick

Give it a chance
For mercy to lance
Be a thoughtful seeker
Not assigned a speaker

No one can ever change
Your curiosity to arrange
Want to discover
Truth to recover

Book of idea pays
Learn curiosity ways
Mental and spiritual thing
Our ability to bring

We stop and smell
Take photos to tell
To be happy
Not at all sappy

Seeker of beauty
Is not just a duty
Learn about the art
See the gallery apart

Beauty to engage
Purges your rage
Learning and seeing
Why beauty is being

J. P. Hughes

See the beauty to be
You can control what you see
You have the control
In taking this role

Have integrity the same
Honest as we claim
Not in flattery
Not insincerity

Not as the sophist taught
Nor with the politician walk
Not a sycophant to praise
In their obsequious ways

Word is bond not to cuss
People now can trust us
Trust is beyond
Love is to belong

Compassionate with charity
Be a nice personality
Take the sermon along
Be a good Samaritan strong

Avoid becoming a skeptic
Thoughts as an epileptic
Love people as you are loved
Not a cynic of that of above

Lyrics of Light

No job, no illness, no test
Will disappointments rest?
No because the happy way
Is not disillusion to convey?

Because you can do all of this
On your own and with your bliss
On the following you depend
This secret of life to send

You are the seeker
You are the curious
You want to know
You seek the beauty

You preserve integrity
You are compassionate
You are nice
You are charitable

None of these depend
On another to defend
This is all up to you
This is what you can do

Build a Tradition

Inspired by an address given by Scott Christensen

Build a tradition
Improve the condition
The secret receipt
Is the work from me

Boys are good cooks
Imperative for looks
To show and sustain
Testimony to remain

Prayer in my heart
Recognize the part
Fingernail tale
Accident to tell

Protected time
Seating remind
Teach about ancestor
Demeanor so sure

Endless to commit
Time to remit
Sacrifice for better
Good living to letter

Lyrics of Light

Teach from the start
This legacy to impart
Plant in your heart
Pray choices as a dart

Live the teaching
Right living reaching
Build faith's dress
Work in progress

See what you have
Sibling time and salve
Jumble of a gift
Relationship lift

Daily prayer
Living aware
Humble self
Not high on shelf

Interact at times
Crisis will remind
Do the right thing
Carry it to bring

Act without fear
Struggling near
No coercion
Forgiving immersion

Step sticking point
Smile and anoint
For hard stuff "Let it go"
Your example show

Buyer Seller

Inspired by my welfare mission

The buyer to receive
The buyer to deceive
The buyer to conceive
The buyer to relieve

The seller to receive
The seller to deceive
The seller to conceive
The seller to relieve

The seller to make
The buyer to take
The seller to shake
The buyer to mistake

The buyer to pay
The seller to stay
The seller to convey
The buyer to say

They want something
To sell or buy or bring
They want an exchange
They want to rearrange

We are the buyer
We are the seller
More than a store
Where we get more

It is the problem for
Expectations to endure
The solution is simple
On a face it is a dimple

The buyer the taker
To respect the Maker
The seller the taker
To respect the Maker

What do you get?
When your life to bet
What do you want
From effort's daunt?

Just "say what you mean"
Just keep it clean
"I have no food"
It is changing my mood

J. P. Hughes

"I cannot pay the rent"
My life is now a dent
"I need some clothes"
For family and those

Buyer be sincere
Not distracting near
Buyer asker say most clear
I will just quit drinking beer

I will not just cover
Deception's cover
I will not deceive
When I receive

The buyer ask
Sincerity's task
The seller
Is the giver

It is for us together
The meaning gather
It is "in compassion's" concern
That this experience I learn

There is no advice
There is no ice
If there is a splice
It would be nice

Lyrics of Light

I can tell you
"What you must do"
You can tell and teach me
More of compassion's plea

And dementia lurks
When nothing works
My effort shirks
Frustration irks

The buyer and the seller
Neither are a retailer
We are both the teller
We are both the seller

Each just want to see
What each other may be
Is it you or is it me?
Is it you or is it me?

Can't Sleep

When you cannot sleep
Dark without a peep
Should I just get up?
Eating, reading to sup

Or lie there to toss?
Turn or get up to floss?

Write down a thought
If any left are sought

Worries to consider?
Problems that make you bitter
Aches and pains
Wind when it rains

Just take a pill?
And stare until
You can drift off
Or get up to cough

Debris

Notice

I noticed that
you noticed
that I noticed
But I didn't think
you noticed
that I noticed.

Distract

Written to distract
From an interest lack

Searching for a fact
Almost asleep intact

Satiation

From our creation
Until our ablation
Searching satiation
From consternation

Demotion

Within our demotion
Lacking our devotion
Living our emotion
Creating our commotion

Desire

It starts with desire
If I may inquire
As one surmised
When it is realized

Results in plain greed
More than any need
No satiation indeed
Or empathy's plead

If desire is not filled
Then anger is spilled
Frustration is tilled
And no one is thrilled

How do we share and dole?
And this desire unroll
Who can just stroll?
When will peace control?

We might not define
Or our position refine
As who we really are
If retired and then afar

Or where we live
No longer can give
Or what we have
No longer a salve

Or what we do
No longer for you
Or what we wear
For looks to share

Or how we speak
Nor seeing a peak
Or just by hearing
Our past now nearing

Or where we have been
Or did or where to begin
Or what people think
Usually gone in a blink

We would take it all
When death makes the call
Away with us forever
No consideration to sever

The truth is that we leave
All that we might believe
With our body and mind
And it is all left behind

We will not take along
Nor scour what used to belong
Just leaving this place
Empty of stuff in space

It all will just stay
And that is the way

Distraction

What is the attraction?
Of our life's distractions
When dividing a faction
From the whole fraction

J. P. Hughes

Why do we divide?
When sitting beside
Where we reside
Cooperation aside

Why distract?
Then attack
Compassion lack
Completion's fact

Memories and Events

My School Eye Exam

"Your little boy is blind"
From our eye test we find
He cannot read
The big "E" a need

"Which way does the "E" point?
First grade teacher would anoint
I did not know
The E did not show

There was no arrow
This exam to blow
I was sent home to fix
Eye and instructions to mix

When I returned
I had now learned
To point my finger
And not to linger

In the direction right
To correspond to sight
But really deep down
When I look around

The "E" still does not direct
Point nor my vision reflect
Which way I now will see
The direction of the big "E"

Biking Back

Biking back
Rain a fact
Lightning and thunder
Bike chain blunder

Metaphor alone
Dark, quiet, no phone

J. P. Hughes

Pushing along my bike
Like when a little tyke

Someone comes along
Fixes chain to wheel belong
Again on my way
Soaked through this day

Now an easy street to shop
Antique's boardwalk drop
Cobblestones and red brick
Shadows breeze moving quirk

Sitting around with friends
Hoping it never ends
Galley restaurant to eat
An event and a treat

Cod, flounder, crab, sea bass
Guatemalan Ishmael with class
Setting sun on the beach
Shadows and colors reach

Visiting and memories
Dessert with plum berries

I Was Lost

    Cabin near home
    Night lost roam
    Changed highway
    Different byway

    I was lost
    Rural cost
    Called on cell phone
    Sitting all alone

    Went way told
    Receptions cold
    Listened with stress
    Not clear confess

    Frustrated to learn
    Rules holy concern
    Music played
    After all conveyed

Convert

    Sweet black face
    Begins from new place
    Soft voices visit
    Our soul to rivet

Friends of good,
Doing what should
Be surely done
For a precious one

Looking across room
Avoiding old and doom
A feeling
For new sealing

You feel it here
The Spirit near
All who came
Never be the same

Distractive thought
Doing what ought
Always occurs
Spirit then it blurs

Just soak it in
From where to begin
It is working
Without our shirking

Exchange

The emphasis is who takes
The essence is who gives

The receiver takes time
Of clothing and toys to find

The giver comes and goes
Slight and quick as the wind blows
Who can ever judge another
In poverty that will smother

One brings in a new sack
Others come to find what they lack
Infant's dark happy eyes move
Looking along a searching groove

Looking for milk bottle to suck
Being here with Mom for luck
Those who take in for need
Now service and help plead

Giver now the helping poor
Smiling, taking, sorting more
Small ones and old
Coming in from the cold

Some here just to return
Others working with concern
Every language spoken
Donations but now a token

Life that is not totally complete
The Creator loves all repeat

Cabin Hammock

Reflecting oak leaf light
Blue sky, white cloud so bright
With the greenish vein
Photosynthesis to gain

Chlorophyll color green
Energy conversion glean
A fly buzzing to land
On my face or writing hand

An ant climbing up the tree
Carrying a load right past me
Sound of a running stream
Distant constant to glean

The sky, the fly, leaf and light
Amazing, "What's not to like?"
Breeze and morning pines
Air power that reminds

Of the seasons
Of the reasons
Many questions why
Answers that make me cry

Eyelids without notice close
Now I sleep with repose
Fading and relaxing
No problem taxing

Butterfly dodging
Squirrel climbing
Bug flying
Robin chirping

Four wheeler grinding
Kids yelling
People talking
Waterfalling

Flatus passing
Parents fleeting
Moments meditating
Day dreaming

Dozing
Snoozing
Unguided thinking
Eyes blinking

Now sitting
Now looking
E. J. working
Rocks stacking

Dead twigs raking
Duck taping
Dirt scraping
Paint flaking

Picking
Packing
Poking
Stacking

Fencing
Leaning
Lifting
Cleaning

Loading
Moving
Puttering
Arranging

Decorating
Collecting
One dreaming
One working

Ingestion

An experience I had while working at the Cottonwood Hospital ER in 1975

As a child
Through life filed
"I swallowed a dead bee"
Not sure it would kill me

"Caught tongue in a lower place"
But could not identify the taste

"Put a bean in my ear"
Made it harder to hear

Tried one "up my nose"
With drainage on my clothes

Put a "Christmas tree ornament"
In my mouth, now no comment

"I have a wood tic in my naval"
Scaring me in the upheaval

A "rectal light globe" placement invited
When I removed it he was delighted

One had a dead "vibrator in there"
To change the batteries "if I did not care"

J. P. Hughes

There was "a thermometer in the bladder"
Lost glass and floating somewhere

One with a miscarriage and barking dogs
"Having contraptions and passing clogs"

Another with "an abstract ball"
A bowel obstruction during ER call

The "meta-musical was not helping"
The constipation straining and yelping

Broken arm diagnostic picture xray
Asked "do I have to smile?" to stay

When asked how did you get here?
She said the "paranautics were near"

One complaint of a swollen belly tender
BM four days ago and now not slender
She said that she also had an ear ache
If they we related what should she take?

The most unusual was at the bank
When I had to sign a check and thank
I pulled out a rectal thermometer
from my shirt pocket then

I will have to go back to the office
"Some bum has my pen"

Phili canum non carborun dum

Flying above the Clouds

    Flying above the clouds
    Some voices talking loud
    Snow white mountain range
    Passing below spaces' exchange

    Sitting on row 33 over the wing
    Stewardess with cookies and nuts to bring
    Aerodynamic miracle to see
    Metal rivets, flaps in harmony agree

    Passing prairie and open space
    Grey earth's cold unspeaking face
    Many here to sleep
    Few taking a little peep

    Hum of the engine constant
    Stream of exhaust to vent
    The experience of us two
    Checking out the view

Silence Sweet

Jennie

Quiet little person talk
Temple measured to walk
Share experience to wait
Why should I consecrate?

I am going to the temple
Three-year-old asked so simple
I walked around this three-year-old
Going to marry me, I was told

Grateful for gospel to leaven
Temple is taste of heaven
I love the ordinances there
Holy love and miracle where

Grateful for His love
Given from above
I can learn and be
The messenger from Thee

Melissa

Love to read the biography
John Adams and geography

Know the story and price paid
All our future at his feet laid

Founding fathers gift
Gratitude to lift
Plan of salvation
From Lord's creation

Story of freedom and liberty
Live with His peace assuredly
Savior came to show the way
Atone for each of us this day

Alison

Power of the scripture read
Quote and talk of God to dead
Tales for me to read
From His teachings plead

Power and force He knows
He loves me the story flows
Grateful for the Savior
What he did I will savor?

Linda

Been here two months now
Grateful for membership's plow
Convert and do all I can
Pay tithing to remand

Righteous in every footstep
In this new ward I crept
Honored to participate
I will concentrate.

Emily

Been in ward forever
It is not being clever
Church on Sunday tag
During the seek I sag

Frustration then temple spirit
When there I still can feel it
Power of testifying sister
Bumbling, doubting time a blister

Church is from God and true
It is wonderful I knew
From my own experience
And the spiritual reliance

Lyrics of Light

Ashley

Thank you for welcoming me in
Got to Salt Lake City to begin
Worship here with you
Little brother in MTC new

It is the most depressing place
Sending my brother's face
Freedom we do enjoy
Our Savior to employee

Margie

Scared to be here and defend
Share a testimony with a friend
Read and pray about this book
Bore testimony to give a look

Laying on hand in the mission
Grateful for worthiness remission
I told her what I believe
Fear and doubt relieve

Todd

Guys we are getting killed
Like jogging and not thrilled

Back into the Church one year
Book of Mormon and new gear

Importance of freedom's say
Book came to me that way
We would not be here now
I love Church and will bow.

Josh

Sitting and thinking about reliance
Seemed comfortable in the silence
Wonderful experience in just coasting
Go to meeting, floating and boasting

Ups and downs, hit bottom low
Climbing out and help me show
Feel love of Savior for me
Strong enough as I pray to Thee

Helped in the hard time
Suffering and bear mine
Frustrated without appreciation
Problems and consternation

So we can struggle and fall
Pick up sorrow best times call
He died in Gethsemane our joy
State of happiness not to annoy

Mariam

From Mexico your love shown
Here now and on my own
Moved here and could not choose
Options where to be and not lose

Happy to be here with you
I can now be and do
Attend or not I decide
Were to be and reside

Prayer every day and read
Scripture answer my creed
Grateful (star earring tingle}
Words spoken slowly jingle

(Standing there
All aware
Love to bear
Testify and share)

Happy to be engaged
Thoughts of happiness rage
Heavenly Father knows me
My heart is full you see

Tinell

Tours and acting pioneer
How treated in this gear
Heard from Brigham Young
Spiritual about freedom

He did not like people
Who drove away the steeple?
Competition to appreciate all
Freedom with trials to fall

Thankful for the gospel free
Perfected and sent from Thee
It is hot at Pioneer Memorial Park
Working there is no lark

Suzanne

Returned from our Israel trip
Place of the sacrificial whip
Spirit spoke and heard
Tombs of pharaohs absurd

The empty simple tomb
Spiritual life everlasting resume
Christ loved them all
The temple and the Fall

Jane

I stand, sit, and kneel to pray
Often times three times a day
Recognize God instrumental
By nature I am grateful

Life is orchestrated by design
Stumbled and fumble to find
My parents got a divorce
As I went on a mission course

I was given a spiritual blessing
My mom left the Church dressing
I could not imagine it for me
Can happen to any you see

Just be faithful and be kind
My mom is back at this time
Bad time in her life
Promise to me in strife

The Lord's hand is in my life
My work is full of strife
Little twins one year later
Picture and note from a crater

Scott

Cell phone text and nudge
From his seat to budge
Dee sent him a part
Of what was in his heart

Stick to your gun
Life is not all fun
Learn it the hard way
Two chances today

Christmas Program

Music of the season muses
Standby for the Hugheses
Beauty of the decorated hall
People sitting wall-to-wall

Tabernacle choir
Singing to inspire
Symphony on Temple Square
Music played with care

Dancers in white
Moving as in flight
Red sashes flow
Undulating as they go

Lyrics of Light

Guest singer stage center
Christmas music Venter
Satin and color red
Steeples and castle fled

Symbol of the lights
In the seasonal sights
Performance for friends
Sharing this choir blends

Entertaining voice
Love animal tunes of choice
Organ with pipes of gold
Sounds vibrate so bold

Poinsettia red leaf
Symbol of our belief
Raised in the dark
Same at this time we park

Then the true color shows
Chlorophyll to root it goes
Lights of the symbolic star
Seen by the shepherds far

Flute, harp, violin, horn
Sound metaphor of child born
Bells hung between wreaths
Symbol of life on the heath

Window lights in square
Warmth of season aware
Snowflake reflections
Winter cold and deflections

Women of the choir in blue
Singing as if to the few
Bell ringers in the aisle
Synchronized with style

Story read at fireplace
Of the new Child's face
It is the time of His birth
For this world and earth

Bishop's History

The 41st Ward, my last six months, 2009

Bishop's history
More a mystery
Sacrament meetings
High council greetings

Linger Longer and fireside
Working and serving beside
Sky and Brighton mountain ski
Robinson's cabin to be

Dinner club and interviews
Ward program with the news
Choir practice and ward mission
Singing, visiting is our commission

Sacrament meeting from our member
Helping Christianity to remember
Classes taught lessons forgot
Relief Society and elders quorum sought

Organizations to change
New members to rearrange
Ward prayer every week
New relationships to seek

Salt Lake, Bountiful, Oquirrh Temples to kneel
Then Draper and Jordon ancestors to seal
Many came to the open house tour
Carpooling, pleading, getting more

Progressive dinner date
With 31st Ward's possible mate
Salvation Army to feed
Two hundred folks in need

41st Ward's sponsor and return
Our full-time missionary's concern
Music presentation of talent love
Filling the soul of peace above

J. P. Hughes

Ward conference as led
By our stake president who fed
"Come Unto Christ"
Our lives to splice

Sacrament passed in silence
Thoughts quiet of our reliance
Organization membership and call
All served standing tall

Ward sacrament program the best
A standard I would suggest
Photo on the front page
Music lyric learning stage

RS Enrichment of food to store
Suggestions, places, ideas, and more
Stake and general authority fireside
Hundreds attending as they preside

Patriarch and blessing
Bishop and confessing
Visiting homes of elderly alone
Stake participation we condone

Ensign mountain hike to peak
Monument, view, and the Spirit seek
Clearing weeds by pulling and kneeling
Lake Bonneville shoreline beauty revealing

Working in the Food Bank
Our own blessings to thank
July's time of our release
Scheduled involvement to cease

Greeting the new man to lead
Friend and high councilman's deed
Dee Darling, John Robinson, and me
Deeply grateful and blessed by Thee

—Bishop J. P. Hughes

Easy Money

If you get easy money
It may not be that funny
It came so fast
But it did not last

More available for a scam
Get rich feeling that I am
Rollover or invest
Lost then I attest

Then there is the blame
The money not to remain
Followed by anger
No fault or danger

Resulting in emotion
Then lack of devotion
Who can you trust?
The bank to bust

It was not just the lie
I asked myself just why?
Did I not take
Not responsibility forsake

It represents hard work
From efforts loss will lurk
It must be a quirk
Easy money to shirk

A Midsummer Night's Dream

After watching the play by William Shakespeare

The depth of this play
May not be for me to say
Do elves and demons direct?
The supernatural to select

Does the dream we have?
Give our mind healing salve
Do we and will we rebel?
What force is to tell?

Where do we explain?
If with a friend remain
We cannot complain
Or at least just contain

Will the confidence betray?
What we say each day
Is our life directed by luck?
Or is it influenced by Puck?

Are we sensitive
Or contemplative?
Do we see with ears?
Do we hear with tears?

Do we appeal
Authority's deal?
Secrets conceal?
Memories reveal?

Was all this effort a farce?
Writing acting words to parse
I think it was deep
Oblique and a mystery keep

Testimonies

Inspired by a talk by Dee Darling

> There is a concept
> Based on a precept
> That the study map for you
> Is not the terrain more true
>
> Meetings are the map
> The terrain is the lap
> Around the track of life
> Visiting the weak in strife
>
> The circumstances different
> The assumptions apparent
> The reality of place
> Is not a pretty face
>
> Sitting, planning, and talking
> It is the working and walking
> The mountain peaks and trail
> Are different when we avail
>
> The valley is low in plain sight
> Plaines are not linear in flight
> Mountain peaks to climb
> Agony but vistas remind

Lyrics of Light

That we share life in common
The trail and walk we summon
Each other back and forth to go
Until we are thru the entire show

Psalm 23—pass through the valley
Of the shadow of death's alley
The valley is in the shadow dark
Blocking out light as an unkind remark

Discouraged and disillusioned lose
The unemployed, bad health choose
Failure, depression, and the long list
Of life and valley's darkest mist

Valley in the shadow blocks the light
Our walk through infested with blight
It may be the valley of the shadow of death
Our prospect of love, and help with breath

Is to walk through, not camp nor stay
The lesson of this life is move on today
Do not homestead nor wallow here
There is light and vision clear

It is possible with a friend
Councilor, physician to end
You are empowered to pass
Possible what learned in class

Heavenly Father is with us
Do not give up all the fuss
The Spirit to comfort and guide
No matter if shadow does reside

Endure to walk through
Comfort strength to you
He will send a servant or friend
We count on never fail nor end

Reality in our soul
His presence our toll
Shared with the Spirit
My heart to His rivet.

Russian Class

Dedicated to Harvey Wilhelm

"We digress"
I must confess
Dance with a cane
Helps me remain

Following as a sick friend
80-pound weight loss end
Still have a bad back
But up out of the sack

Have chemo brain
Memory to fain
It is all in there
But find it where?

Design homemade
Sets of tapes fade
Review of Russian
Sounds of concussion

Video and sound
Has book compound
Video tape to DVD
Digitized better to see

Russian class tonight
Might learn in spite
Bot casa word
Might sound absurd

Peter Ustenoff died
2004 multilingual spied
Connection to German why?
Russian Army as a spy?

Do not pronounce in French
Terminal consonants
Bear and beer except
Only word to respect

He was born 1910, let's say
He died in 2002 at 94 today
He had a great accent
The video history vent

Harry was at Monterey
Learning the Russian way
Take a closer look
He taught and forsook

Now on the Federal grand jury
18 months and in no hurry
Fun and got to substitute
District plan to refute

Chemotherapy was tough
No hair loss but rough
Just now a wave
Then chemo behave

Loss of energy this dynamo
Hard to get up you know
I.V. Rotuxin , $24,000 charge
Seems quite high and large

Lymphoma responds to save
All bad cells now in their grave
Cyber knife target area's way
In 2 millimeter radium spray

Lyrics of Light

Lighting in the abyss
Like a step to miss
Blessing in disguise
Until my demise

Rating the truth now moves
To get form chaos it behooves
Optimistic and not to dwell
Now I feel calmness swell

Third grandson of Fredonia
We are on way to Arizona
808-7763. BTW say
Meaning "by the way"

Generation cannot spell
Semi-literate as well
Retired from school
Stressed work a fool

Online not to learn or say
About Merle K. Shumway
Taught me the grammar
Notebooks in full manner

Cannot leave "this pet peeve"
Form plural apostrophe then leave
Never use an apostrophe to form
A personal possessive to conform

Cat licks its paw
Apostrophe in English saw
Possessive for noun
Not ever as a pronoun

Contractions like I'm
Do not and don't
Lift out a letter
Might sound better

I, me, my, personal pronoun
My or mine possessive found
Thou, Thee, Thy, Thine, the same
Kept it straight and still remain

Pre-postrophy
For the apostrophe
He, him, his to have
No comma salve

We, us, ours, in genitive
She, her, her, hers retentive
Fall on sword may be objective
It, is same as: he, she, in nominative

You, you, your, yours, you're
Is a contraction for you are
Your welcome needs apostrophe
Your not possessive without, you see

Indonesian with no gender
To mess up linguistic fender
Jakarta word the *capol* is boat
Anok is child, *anock* many float

Three thousand Islands
Ketab is book of Arabic lands
Muktab is the library
Easy language but contrary

They, them, their, theirs,
Growing old in underwears
Plural noun apostrophe end
Got lost and had to send

Na taxi, Moshna meaning
Possible indeclinable seeming
Coffee, kangaroo as well
Get it straight is swell

Transformation grammar
Russian conversation assure
I like ice cream aspect slur
Form, verb or not, to blur

Numbers are genitive plural
Of nominative that is the rule
Evade your eyes
No, not plagiarize

Change element places
Sparkling new faces
Be inventive
And creative

Giving incentive
Hopefully retentive
Advantage out of head
Copy what you have read

Conversation on every level
Correct this Russian devil
Sound like a Russian booking
Going through without looking

Suppose you are a tourist
Ask what to do to rest
Dot not feathers
India for druthers

Islam, *Asia Times* online
Spengler wrote about it fine
Occasionally lays an egg
But no one has a perfect leg

Mustard seed in national affairs
Why irrational he compares
Regensburg learned assembly called
Catholic theologians installed

Benedict 16th cardinal Joseph Ratzinger
Conclusion was a humdinger
Was doctrinal orthodoxy to enforce?
John Paul II Polish, Karl Voteva of course

In God's name John Paul the first
Read and 34 days was dead and worst
Metnet Ali Aza, Turk Bulgarian SST
Shot the Pope who visited him, see

Solution to problem in ice
Convert Moslem to Christ
Sharia law from Archbishop of Canterbury
About did in Anglican problem gay raspberry

77 million in Providence of Nigeria with concern
By conservative force rallied to discern
Will African Christians raze Mecca made?
Will Europe raise this decay now displayed?

Moslems, Arabs captured the Nigerian slaves
To sell to England, brought to America from caves
When he is bad he horrid new
Spengler cynical about global view

Iran demography birthrate collapse
Worse than in Europe immigration relapse
Crippled by nature, now fossilized by it
No dialogue, logic, or reason in the circuit

Jihad movement reaction to doom
A culture fighting in a lost cause loom
Casualties after Vicksburg, Gettysburg's victory steeple
Defeat assured but more lives lost and death of people

Sherman clearest thinker to kill 300,000 for a village
Best march seen through Georgia without rape and pillage
We can learn, discern, and have concern about his burn
But how do you resolve, evolve, involve, and absolve?

LDS General Conference

Thoughts I had while waiting in line for general conference

> Doors open at eight-thirty
> Could sleep and get pretty
> Enter any gate
> I can appreciate
>
> No cell phone
> Received a moan

Lyrics of Light

No photo camera
No record panorama

Met a patient volunteer
Discussed fistulae clear
Sat on balcony row
Front seat I know

See and partake
Of choir practice take
Mack Wilberg there
Red dresses declare

Samoan blocked drive
Came late to arrive
Pull in back I said
He blocked all instead

This conference hall
Inspires us all
I am glad to be here
To feel Spirit near

Time to spend
Until the end
Frozen outside
Warmer in confide

J. P. Hughes

Pioneers did not have it this bad
To stand and freeze like we had
To wait one hour
They had all the power

People filing in
Past doors of tin
We will meet after
I called from rafter

Sitting here alone
Strange feeling zone
People hard to please
Ushers will not tease

Distinguished by rank
Our hope now sank
Levels of richer
Relegated pitcher

Chance to learn
More rank to earn
Ignore the poor
Poverty for sure

Learning because rich reside
Lifted up in their pride
Humble not revile, abide
Ranking now put aside

Lyrics of Light

Church broken up
By the judgment cup
Great inequality in land
Most departed as the sand

Some few immovable
Steadfast irrefutable
Most stirred and puffed up
Simple life most corrupt

Seeking more power
In immediate hour
Want more authority
Show my superiority

Vain things of world
Around head curled
Hearts led away
Few in Church to stay

Did not ignorantly sin
They knew the truth within
They had been taught
And knew what they sought

They willfully rebel
The present story I tell
Lawyers anger to judge
From evil would not budge

Secretly put to death a few
Knowledge of those judges knew
People complained about the law
Taken and injustice they saw

Judge's lawyer friend
What they did had no end
United by family kin
Never considered it sin

Entered in a covenant
Old administered respondent
Combined against all good
This will stop and should

Combined to destroy
Life and every toy
Grasp of justice lost
Murder is OK with a cost

Funeral of E. R. McKay

What can you say?
About Ed McKay
My mentor and friend
My specialty to send

I loved his example
My life to sample

Sitting here reflecting
Old memories deflecting

He had a presence
A dignity of essence
He stood tall
And was kind to all

I worked on his service
Medical rounds not nervous
He had a smile
That will last a while

He was the gentleman
A goal set for all that can
He had infectious love
Given to one from above

His children became
And still remain
Close to him their father
Always one they could bother

Edward

He was sick for one month now
Congestive heart to plow
He died in his recliner
Watching tennis open finer

J. P. Hughes

He played tennis to show
His serve and return flow
His friends to play
Few of them stay

"Imagine the grim reaper
Black cloak, scythe," and beeper
"Coming to get my Dad
Afraid to tell Lottie who is sad"

Many old friends attend
His viewing and life's end
Many of a medical world past
It obviously never will last

Hard to recognize
An old face surprise
From years of training
40 years ago few remaining

He was such a good guy
We loved him and cry
There is such a short time
Ninety-two years remind

After an incredible prayer
Thoughts deep conveyer
Life sketch then read
About the living dead

He decided at five
A doctor will arrive
Help the patient ills
No credit for his skills

"Your father saved my life"
When in sickness and strife
Many could not afford
Never cancelled on board

"You should not be"
I'm not concerned and see
Treatment is not science
Kindness for reliance

He gave us a Sprite
When sicknesses fight
Apparently he was right
When given at night

Huntsville home love
Happiest family dove
Gathered for a good time
Horse ride remind

Follow him to ride
Catch, saddle, bridle confide
Earn right to ride a horse
Tried alone of course

Daisy in dry hollow revision
Horse not share the same vision
As a nine-year-old rider
Bucked off beside her

Put back in the saddle
No complaints or prattle
Do not ever give up
Great lesson not corrupt

He loved to travel
Intense study unravel
Culture, history, and tradition
Perfect guide for condition

Chose natural disaster places
War, hurricane, earthquake spaces
He relished the confliction
Traveled Egypt affliction

"This is a part of history"
He relished the mystery
Sirens going off and stand
By sandbags in desert land

Took continuing education at the U
No exams but the work he knew
All he did was in grace
Humility in honor's face

John

Grateful that you came
Sister is an angel same
Always at his side
Passed her care abide

"He was very nice"
Best of any funeral advice
From a grandchild's talk
With grandpa to walk

Bless her heart
To do her part
Note to myself
"Utah Man" on shelf

At the Swiss Temple aware
Spirits were really there
Feeling so strong where
"My Dad was there"

Words of his prophet dad
Lifted his heart and was glad
Sacred loved one
By side will come

Impossible to describe
Knew him beside

He was the greatest
Not just the latest

Gratitude for life and powers
Stop and look at the flowers
Seed, water, and sun
Work until sunset is fun

He had focus
Crescendo for us
It was a selfless treat
Whenever we meet

Always giving not hide
Treat word or confide
Money to give and care
Work ethic" just do it" aware

Love of garden and life
Brought tarantula strife
He brought it to our home
From the road to roam

He had a great sense of humor
Even on a naval destroyer
He told a POW's appendicitis
Removed if he did not fight us

Everything would be alright
He had seen once to help
Cursing and lurching sure
Ether never given before

"He's under now" told
Better operate so bold
"Vergatz zar goot"
"More ether to boot"

Not quite so much
Watching detail as such
He wrote "My love, sweetheart
You are my life yet apart"

He was unassuming
Lived it no lecture looming
Vibrant spirit is free
Real as life can be

Hailed friends with joy
Rejoiced to see them toy
With life of happiness
Sincerity of his caress

Apostle Monson long ago
Came to see a missionary glow
In Germany he did greet
President McKay's grandson's treat

J. P. Hughes

It was a tribute to my dad
Inconvenience was all he had
He had turned around
And then me he found

The bishop asked
Of a long life basked
Without hesitation
Chocolate digestion

President Monson

I read words a life gone
Voice stills place to long
All now in a Spirit home
Lives today eternities roam

I was on BYU board
U of U not in accord
David O. McKay asked
What is the serious task?

I love both schools
Will not have rules
He told me that day
Basketball you do not play

45 years ago he called me
As an apostle to see

Where have 45 years gone
Shown that time marches on

He had a painting on the wall
Of gift Huntsville home and all
She had painted the wrong one
He hung it just the same as done

ERM called me
On the phone to see
Talk how's today?
I have stuff to say

He talked about his life
Family, hereafter, and strife
Premonition of the end
Two-hour visit with a friend

That was the last time
I saw him alive to find
A family of truth and joy
A prophetic success to employ

He walked in truth and light
He was my doctor, very bright
He was gentle and nice
He saved in surgery and advice

"Before formed I knew thee"
Spirit departs and returns to Me
Rest from sorrow
Time here to borrow

Rest from all care
Eternity is over there
Rest from the storm
Paradise is now born

How will it be found?
Loved ones all around
They will case it out
When we arrive about

Look for the best
Find it and all the rest
Stay close to your mother
Greater love has no other

"Son, behold thy mother"
Mother, behold thy Son"
Make sure she has a smile
Husband united in a while

"I will not leave you
Comfortless with few"
You have family forever
The ties firm as a lever

Galapagos

One to three million years
Bird beaks different cheers
Started from one bird
Kind of seems absurd

All but one present now live
From what God started to give
Study each offspring size
To survive we surmise

Larger from original adult
To survive draught's assault
Sever El Niño with storm
Water poured to new alarm

Measure growth of plant each day
Growth rings from 1983 the way
Finches breed for ten months
With eight chicks nest blunts

Then conditions change
Smaller now the need rearrange
Small feed supply now gone
Starvation and death's gong

Shift and reverse with environment
The average adaptation not in cement

Great stress causes change now
Darwin never saw again somehow

Exploration with question in storm
Why, how do species form?
Music and photography feel
Deeper meaning to seal

Tomorrow what will happen?
To Iceland to hear Eric Clapton
Blue-footed booby flies
Deep tour of water sighs

How can you write?
About such a sight
An example of how life does begin
And those adaptive survival win

The tourist who goes
Already Galapagos knows
It is a dream comes true
Even boobies with feet so blue

The volcanic origin of all
Tectonic plates separating fall
Gives earth's core magma rise
An access to rolled lava's surprise

Fissures of molten and broken crack
Water and volcano meet with smack
Seams from the land drift
To vegetate this new rift

Sacrament Meeting

Ann

John 21:15–17

Feed my sheep, said Thee
Love me times three
Do unto least
This is my feast

Love brother and sisters
Feed by service blisters
Inconvenient patience
Discouraged compliance

Spreadsheets screen lure
Find the small and obscure
Little old lady lost her car
Remember color, type, far

Felt horrible wondering
Rain dripped sundering

Annoying, but felt good
Helping elderly should

Cindee

Limping to pulpit
Crutches permanent
Personal choices
Acted by others

Choose you this day
Do not turn anyway
Kids grew up
So far so good, sup

Avoid temptation's evil
Alma 56:46 to reveal
Taught by their mothers
They knew it all brothers

Important the very most
Who is married the host?
Affects way to live
And much to give

I got him this way
Hysterical today
Mutual beehive
Girls hard to revive

Lyrics of Light

I did not know this
Away off to kiss
Stopped going at all
Friend begged to stall

I want to have
Husband to salve
Awful dorm
Not the norm

I called normal sane
Moved here on the train
Do remember Harold?
Blind date, caroled

Go back to find
Personal choir remind
Make choices and change
Our life to rearrange

Observe and be fruitful
Live life more truthful
Just make better decision
A better life is revision.

Choir

Choir to sing
Flute to ring

Piano sound
Spirit around

Voices of men
Messages send
Sounds of high
Woman singing cry

Together sing all
With piano flute tall
Lyrical flow
Spirit to know

Harold

Bias for musical number
Rebuttal to spiritual slumber
Blind date with a Hughes
From Southern CA news

Color of eyes brown
Mine all blue around
Asked her to go out
Now 14 grandkids shout

Her dominate brown
Many ways I've found
Speak about blessing
Read more confessing

Father's Day now reside
Patriarch means father beside
Blessing from God to guide
Worthy of it confide

Article of Faith six
Importance we fix
Evangelical minister
Is a patriarch rector

Joseph Senior was first one
Then Brother Hyrum bless some
Lehi and journey's gift
Historic voyage's lift

Round ball of brass
Spindles for this class
Direction to life
Safe passage's strife

Personal treasure
Revelation measure
Voice of utterance
Source in abundance

Give lineage list
Family tribe bliss
Entitled and seal
God will reveal

Authority to seal
Blessing most real
Humbling to me
From Lord to see

Not fortune teller drift
Must labor for this gift
Divine goal to send
Power of lives amend

Anchor in cloudy days
Guide our life new ways
Not talk or shown
Distinctively known

Sacred and private
Parental idea revive it
Carried past the vale
Along the married trail

His timing not ours
Receiving these flowers
Called of God's power
Blessing given this hour

Love and compassion
Try to be in fashion
Of this patriarch faithfully
Not own wisdom especially

Lyrics of Light

Nor any training
The spirit remaining
Receiving instruction
Humble construction

Guidance and comfort
From scriptures report
Not just getting by
One shot deal rely

Blessing from Lord is right
From your spiritual insight
Given in thoughtful prayer
The source deeply aware

Enoch to preach
Heard prophecy teach
Eyes that do not see
Heart waxed for Thee

Why have I favor?
Slow of speech, Savior
But a lad at sixty-five years
No man please with spears

Give and worry
Words come in hurry
Spirit of Lord dictates
Total stranger reiterates

J. P. Hughes

Know God truly loves us
Now I understand the fuss
Blessing from world
People lost and hurled

Listened to Him
Story of life's rim
Not my decision
His life revision

Abraham study life still
Willing to subject his will
Posterity, priesthood, promise
Not for a Doubting Thomas

Blessing of gospel remain
Same blessing sustain
Declaration if the same
It is true and will remain

Got it as Liahona new
Blessing is for you
Life choices not same
Ask it in His Name.

Temple Session

Bry Badger

Temple session
Brother concession
New in this call
Good to see you all

Change in time and place
Good to see your face
Life-long quest to end
1838 tithing D&C 119 send

Land will be sanctified
Buildings dotting justified
All we do points to the gift
Endowment, covenant lift

Enter into His presence
Symbolic His residence
He gave His Son complete
His teachings here replete

Plan of happiness is taught
Examples of love He bought
Peace and forgiveness He gave
Obedience and our reliance save

J. P. Hughes

Peace I leave and give
A better way to live
Last Supper "I Am" with you
Follow me after if you are true

Not lifted without a Comforter
Savior promised consolateur
Feel this Spirit evident of love
Fills this place from above

We know source of all
Savior in New World call
Mission light life to see
Finally come unto me

Slain for the sins, then depart
It is a manner of the heart
Testify and come unto Savior
Invitation to worship's flavor

Sister Lewis

Sister Lewis to share
Cooking and child care
Fat grouse hit the window
Led by friend affection show

Injured bird shockingly stood
Chirping strident friend could

Wow of a caring in nature
Love by any other creature

For this cause He taught
The gift that He bought
We can learn though dead
The injured soul to shed

President Lewis

Returned from mission sight
Find, teach, challenge, invite.
We connect with the temple
Spirit teaches by example

Techniques of the mission
Date, referral, blind commission
Invite to marry in teaching pool
Not just for fun or to be cool

Come unto Christ, not another
Find someone to come together
Holy Ghost and testimony grew
Have strength and come anew

Get married in strange condition
Date and come to temple rendition
Invite and take into the font
Her response will you daunt

Why would I go—wow
Right kind of spirit now
Catch a glance and look
The Spirit important shook

Ponder, meditate, and pray
In celestial room stay
Finish baptistry in the chapel
Teach and bear heart's grapple

Burning bosoms, trumpet blow
Who do I marry and how
I spoke peace in mind and heart
Spirit of revelation impart

Temple center as led along
Spirit of temple veil and song
Look about for a purpose
Success is not on surface

This is the Lord's university
Edified by teaching diversity
Celestially ponder, prove, and pray
Ask if we should marry this day

You already hold and have your answer
Neither burning bush nor whirlwind dancer
More in the stillness of your heart
Smile and appreciate your part.

Sacrament Meeting Mother's Day

Mark Browning

Born the first and only son
When home from school no fun
Mother school teaching
I was blue, cold and reaching

Discovered a heart with a hole
Life in development control
Need surgery to close
Heart holes I suppose

Idaho to SLC for operation
22-month-old cooperation
Tube broke in my heart
Open surgery again impart

Mom told me
Stories to see
Problems as a teen
Mom not happy seen

Brought mom a card
Life without her hard
Donate first for child
Husband now not wild

Mercy of the Lord
Love in family accord
More tables turn
She had a stroke, we learn

Needs a heart transplant
Donation from family can't
Change of life
Now with strife

Serve my mother
As no other
Cheerfully accept
Heart recovery attempt

Sick post-op
Doctor to shop
Feeble of mind
Child to remind

Comprehension not sure
Coma infection lure
Cleared up at home
Teachers again roam

You are pretty young
Andy hand clapped sung
Crying and lost
Time with me cost

Sit next to me
Draw me a story, see
Stack of pictures hang
"Skubeedo" art we sang

He died alone
She sat to moan
Love God heart, strength, and mind
Love neighbor easy to find

If say love God
Love brother abroad
He washed my sin
Away Lord forgive

Jesus, I can and will forgive
My heard healed and I live
Savior loves us deep
Even as we sleep

"For God so loved the world"
He spread a gospel unfurled
Scriptures will guide
Setting life aside

Suzanne and Mom

Great qualities of Mom to seek
Primary song then to speak

Lead back to Heavenly Father
Parents loved the Lord, no other

Mother lenses to see
Life and God with thee
Mother kneeling each day
Bows her head to pray

Mother prays below steeple
Prophet pray for people
Christ prayed for us
Search, ponder, and fuss

Listen to this
"Gives me a kiss"
Loves to see temple
Placed for an example

Worked together for a while
Best friend for her smile
Sister and I are going there
Special time to share

Daily active service
Child of God not nervous
Teach all I must do
We must act for you

Do this for one
"Giving tree" some
Tree loves boy
Cut down toy

I need quiet place
To me death's face
Mom adjust and grown
Now teach not moan

Pauline

Primary teacher and song
Teach us all so long
My mother rich was not
Her fame never sought

She had a follower's part
Lived with a true heart
Lived in a log cabin no lock
Then Coleville built of rock

Ten cents an hour job
Grateful for the lob
Taught piano lessons
Playing for concessions

Ward organist and then
The oldest of ten

J. P. Hughes

Job insecurity roam
Sent money home

Widow with six
One on mission fix
Worked hard on farm
Dad died with alarm

I was a five-year-old
Mom was 43 and bold
Fear gripped her heart
No job to impart

Job in a band
Cared by hand
No welfare money sad
Lived on what we had

Mom's windows were open now
Tithing blessings somehow
She listened to prophet McKay
She had a two-year supply

It was a comfort for me
Plenty of food you see
My uncle had a farm
Filled a large freezer arm

Lyrics of Light

Grew up in Park City
As a bright seed
Hoytsville for work
Plant, harvest not shirk

Put up pears and corn
Midweek help adorn
With the harvest food
200 chickens in brood

Harvests then chickens clean
Gross me out with the spleen
I did my part contribute
Then at the end distribute

Mom never had a credit card
Or would have any idea hard
No one ever used one
Paid tithing when done

Saved a percent of income
Then bought with cash some
Never used any credit tug
Always droved a VW bug

Saved money to buy
Three kids asked why
Never go to Ensign Downs
Feel sorry for the clowns

J. P. Hughes

Buy only what you need
Different wants now indeed
Brother and a new car
After you have money far

Mom played at 7:30 pm more
Snyderville farm work before
She taught me music to play
I have used it to this day

We walked to church alert
She was totally the convert
Take the sacrament true
Had a calling until ninety-two

Every member calling jam
She set aside folded program
Fractured hip at ninety-one
Visiting teacher until done

Never wait but made time
Planned to do it in rhyme
Foundation of the Church
Accommodated not lurch

Door always open to all
Welcome to big or small
Remarkable and steadfast
Quiet attention to last

Be thou humble
Submissive not tumble
Easily entreated
Temperance greeted

My memory to treasure
Broken arm and hip measure
That night at my bed
Kneeling prayers she said

Ray Liddell

What can you tell?
About Ray Liddell
Kind and goodly man
Surgical helping hand

A general father as he grew
Moving made friends anew
When married, had a girl and boy
Energy, love, enthusiasm, and joy

He taught school at SLCC
Surgical assistants to click
Working in the operating room
Challenge of excellence resume

He worked at St. Mark's for years
His thoughtful order it appears

His efforts with a smile
Deep voice speaking style

This honor and award
Is given truly toward
A good and steady man
Who lives the best he can

Mickey Hansen

Family program
Almost musical jam
For Mickey Hansen
Senior home dancing

Jess deaf in her right ear
Harp playing leaning near
To the elderly hair white
Sounds of solace this night

Entertained to honor her
Miki friend so dear
Soft strings playing of sound
Hard to not just look around

Memories of the past
We thought they would last
Her children looking on
With elderly lives almost gone

Our grandchildren sitting there
Quietly listening to share
Playing "I Am a Child of God"
On the guitar to applaud

Ten years old
Standing so bold
Sterling played softly
Small but lofty

Elaine's memorization of Sam McGee
Reading given about Tennessee
The presentation was by my loving E. J.
Three days after Christmas day

It was touching
To see Mickey clutching
To an ancient memory
Her tears now temporary

Now she is living at Sarah Daft
Clean and kind with no draft
Her family home at 137
Was her earthly heaven

We share this place
Looking into her face
And have great respect
Our own memories to reflect

Carmen

The opera, where to begin
By poet in Russia, Puskin
He had never seen a bullfight
But had the conquest right

Sometimes we are the bull
Fighting and strength so full
Sometimes we are the matador
The one we all adore

The metaphor of the military
Order and control for all to see
Yet José, matador of this military rank,
For love, lust, and power, his control sank

He was now the bull
His strength so full
The exchange of places
With the changing of faces

Puskin made José the bull
Fighting, killing now so full
He then, as the crowd jeers,
Kills Carmen because of his fears

He could not force
Nor control her course

She was now the toreador
Loving and asking for more

Yet now she was the bull
Killed for sure lust so full
The players and energy
Music, word, and synergy

Theme of despair
Our roles so aware
Yet the soldier is a fool
The killing was the tool

Showing the audience
Who then in suspense
Who controls a gypsy free?
Clap and check death to see

To extend the hope
But tightening the rope
The play is deep
The secrets keep

The opera Carmen
Is a metaphoric blend
Puskin had it right
All of us are in a fight

We are never the same
Our roles will not remain
We often change to one
Then transition is done

Carol Lee

A homily in tribute to Carol Lee, given by an Episcopal priest, which he entitled "She gave us her life"

Loved and now return
Friends with concern

Realized what was done
Smiling always fun
Knew about so much
Kind and humor touch

Not bored when retired
Listen to trials inspired
Loved to joke with you
Kept the peace so true

You never know
Best time to show
What do you say?
Of this sorrow's day

Best people to know
In her grace to show
She is now gone
Not lost till dawn

She was a theme
Guiding with a gleam
If challenging a friend
Her voice would defend

She is Part of you
She is Part with you

Continue her memory
Who we are in reverie

"Her humor
Her honesty
Her truth
Her compassion
Her value
Her voice
Her story"

Carry the legacy
Full to capacity

None to replace her
Our emotions stir

Until memories blur
Now we all concur

Mike

I had a paper route
Biking early a.m. about
Had feelings of clout
Need as adult no doubt

Four Years Old

After spending two days
With a grandkid who plays
Ava with all honesty
And me with sensitivity

Asked her mother quietly
Others listening slightly

"What is Grandma Elaine's
Husband's name?"

Ghana Child

The men dig a pit
For the sewage to fit

Women carry rocks
On head with socks

This volunteer project
Small village detect
Hookworm to prevent
Stepping in pool's decent

Bathroom near the school
Before long walk to fool
They would not come back
Then education to lack

Medical student group
Studies of food and poop
Fifty students in public health
Project with abstract of wealth

Publications to read
More of the internet to feed
All started with a child
With malaria sick and wild

An infant to cure
Entire village sure
Gratified to come
The Chief part of some

Malaria diagnosis blood test
Barekuma population the rest
Seventy-six percent under five
Six percent to try and survive

What triggers the sick?
Ten percent red blood cells to pick
Mosquito bite and parasite
Goes to the liver to fight

Medicines would not kill
Recurrent problem still
Cloriquin pill to treat
Killing parasite is neat

Five hundred million per year
One million die each to fear
Daniel Anson developed a vaccine
Not perfect in six months was seen

Sporozoan in thirty minutes will daze
Living in the red blood cell phase
Radiation of the male Anopheles'
Reduction of the mosquito please

Nana Tibiri is the Chief
His grandson received relief
The Golden Stool was hidden
Seeing it was forbidden

In this same village
The British desire to pillage
To find this stool
And not be the fool

This stool came from heaven
This Chief walks with leaven
To lift his tribal people up
For generations not corrupt

Harp Music

Music from harp strings
The spirit of soul springs
Played by the Muses
Our Welsh symbol uses

Original a bow and string
One hunter listening sing
Then added one more
A lyre sounds so sure

Sounds of a child playing
Thoughts of me saying
"This little nine year old"
Sitting plucking bold

It makes a grandpa proud
Hearing child's choir cloud

Harp music soft and loud
Incredible performance endowed

La Bohème

After watching Giacomo Puccini's 1896 opera put on at Pioneer Memorial Theater

On Christmas eve
Landlord deceive
Poet and musician
Painter and philosopher man

Marcello will show
Burning pages of Rodolfo

Priesthood Executive Meeting

An angel's face
In the meeting place
Youth in water risen
Report of a baptism

Song and a prayer
List of names aware
Reserve list
No one missed

Action report of eleven
Service effort of heaven
Secretary and clerks
No one here shirks

A spiritual thought
Of the Lord's spirit sought
Conference talk review
Teaching something new

Each in room of commission

Young men
New ones send
Elders quorum
Home teaching some

High priest group of each
Specific people to reach
Relief Society sister
Kindness as a specific lifter

Been to the home
Knows where kids roam
The specific name
Of reaching the same

Problems discussed
Learning fussed

Discussion in fun
House, illness, new babies done

"Last Man Out"

Dedicated to Luis Urzua

"The last man out"
The world's shout
Scenes of celebration
Of rescue elevation

Capsule thrill
Percussion drill
33 men to save
Each fought brave

San Jose mine
Chile miracle divine
Watching wonderment
Trapped but content

"We all are well"
Never the same to tell
Safely brought
Gratefully sought

69 days under ground
Leadership bound

Who will be free?
Amazing thing to see

Thoughtful rescue
Minute detail too
Mission complete
Chilean success repeat

Standing tall for all
National holiday this fall
All thirty-three
Brought to safety

August 5, 2010, onset
So long not to forget
Rebirth by far
Family spectacular

Family always here
Bringing all a tear
Horns, cars, and lights
Bells and church sights

Medical expertise
Problems to please
With God we are not alone
In this earthquake of stone

This was the right way
Hope and happiness today
The shift supervisor
Was the one to inspire

A person of respect
Belief and hope to inject
All people gave all
Chilean support to the call

Will never be the same
Buried and not to blame
New value in the blessing
Ended mystery and the guessing

Unity, faith, and loyal
Was the success's goal
Chile confront the great
Of any challenge or fate

The emotion within
Price of life so thin
"I was excited and proud"
Celebrations out loud

It is in the heart
Bells now impart
Responsible to improve
Life digging in a groove

"Look" at the emotion'
Of workers in devotion
Lessons to lead
All countries plead

Hear of the world best
Thanksgiving to the rest
"Depth of earth"
Emotions of worth

Discipline was strong
Achievement long
Family kiss
Treasure not to miss

Super Mario demand
Luis shift foreman
Passed a small note
Of a message connote

"We are all well"
Deep within we tell
We keep our purpose in routine
We keep working in the seam

We kept the 12-hour shift
Moving dirt off a cliff
We kept a level head
We rationed in this dread

Until the "last man to leave"
Then we could all believe
We had seen a miracle
Hope is now universal

Chilean president was there
Sebastian Pinere was aware

So many feared lost
Find them at any cost
Joyous ending
Message sending

Raised from depth
At surface all wept
All trapped and survived
Last man arrived

Twenty-hours operation
Flawless devotion
"We have done what the world was waiting for"
The spirit of God and grace to endure

President Sebastian Pinera gave tribute
To courage patience cooperation as music's flute
Right arm held high
From all who did try

Answers of prayer agree
In the faces of thirty-three
Seventy days not in vain
A response of all who came

Heart and tears to remain
Life not death complain
"You are not the same"
"You are not the same"

Tears of joy and tears
Faces of each appears
For families we fight
Brought to surface this night

Our anthem to sing
After safety we bring
Each miner to hoist
Each miner eyes moist

Celebration at Camp Hope
Confetti, balloons on mountain slope
Spontaneous cheer
As each miner came near

World and neighbors waiting
World and neighbors contemplating
Horns honking, people yelling
This life of joy swelling

J. P. Hughes

Flags slogans horns blowing
World seeing and knowing
Teary eyed
Because all tried

"Eyes of a transfixed globe"

Welcome to life"
Rescued from strife
Phoenix capsule rescue
Of all thirty-three to view

Painted white and blue
Colors of Chilean flag too
Pod lowered below
The collapsed 700 ton flow

Rescue men let down
To explain to the found
Rescue plan with care
On top and below aware

Brought up from the dark
Lights waving so stark
They were clean shaved
All involved well behaved

Rescued men led a cheer
Of all those standing near

San Lorenzo the patron saint
When arose there was no complaint

"As if born again"
A new life to begin
Captivated by endurance
Unity work and assurance

"I was born a miner"
My rescue was divine
9:55 p.m. at age fifty-four
Luis Alberto Ursua's conture

Tight rations to survive
Limited food to deep alive
Kept shifts working
Not one shirking

"We hope that all Chile shows its strength to help you get out of this Hell"

COMMUNITY AND POLITICS

Leed

    Granola, tie-dyed it seemed
    Big companies support beamed
    Environmentalist cavort
    Go green now to support

    Impact on greenhouse gas
    Presentation teach to pass
    Saudi oil embargo '70s jobs
    None available for many sobs

Lyrics of Light

Integrated design for all
Electrical, mechanical call
Utah Olympic oval to go
Build and the world marvel

Make the ice fast
Building beauty last
Collaborative effort
Preservation character report

Escalante science center
Design process ecology renter
Kennecott visitor for copper
Design of sustainable hopper

BLM at Gateway is example
Internal consultant studio sample
Draper Library functional beam
Tamarack Village stealth green

Holistic site water material energy
Saving indoor quality synergy
Meet with owner occupier stake
Ideas listed with process make

Collaboration communication
Project our sublimation
Alteration and transformation
Bike lanes substantiation

Reused materials, natural paint
Save and use construction saint
Get good view of window light
Will lift the work, Spirit in sight

Big problem in carbon dioxide lint
Coal-fired carbon footprint
Building use 50% of this energy
Auto use 28% in its way surgery

Electricity is 70% problem us mine
Reduce GHG emissions of time
Utah temp is up 2 degrees, idea fluent
Make the building more efficient

Wind-generated power equal
To goal of coal-fired sequel
Photo sensor with the sun
Nevada could provide a ton

Reduction standard is goal
Carbon neutral 30% with coal
The ideas were discussed
The implications missed

Heating water with solar source
Makes a lot of sense, of course
Appraiser, banker gives more value
USGBG professional engineer fallow

Incentive square foot tax
Utah clean energy credit facts
Silver gold points to grade
At least 17% improvement made

Rotary

Inspired by an address from Mark Gibbons

Avoid out of respect
Not a friendly aspect
Never get to know
Would never show

Any nod of greeting
At any meeting
Not personal about me
Just occupied, you see

Retail department store
Construction for more
Nordstrom and Macy's built
Ground and fill in the silt

Designed desirable outside
Slides for kids to reside
Glass built into the store
So we can see more

J. P. Hughes

A hundred stores to see
900,000 feet to be
Convertible roof
Retail not aloof

Bad weather cover
Shoppers to hover
The people not to smother
Retractable roof for another

Open 70% of the year to attract
Keep them shopping then retract
Leadership and design
Saving on energy fine

Environmental design or LEAD
Not built for construction speed
Skybridge store connector
Over the Light Rail connector

Line of restaurants not small
Staring at the new waterfall
Open plaza to Galivan' store
City Creek overseeing more

Destruction, revocation being
The local economy will sing
Secret of our management
Helping people concentrate

A way for the undecided
Living accommodation resided
Downtown construction rising
Revitalize the city surmising

Shorter walking distance, open space
Integrated inner city grid's new face
200 resident housing bids
Not really comfortable for kids

Demolished phase at present
Not yet construction sent
ZCMI food court remains
35,000 tons material contains

Excavation is 50 feet deep
4 levels parking below to keep
Demolition almost complete
Start foundation repeat

5000 stalls to park
All below ground in dark
No backing out to move
Pull out on road behoove

Six acres of green space
City creek recycled face
Vegetation and cobble street
South Temple walks to meet

Fountains with great art
Interactions then depart
Office building in 4 towers
For money people powers

Office remains for Key Bank
Floors converted to thank
Food court below
Courtyard people flow

700 residential homes aware
Now south of Temple Square
Different water features
For the people creatures

20 stories in another tower
Now being built by crane power
Condos 2012 completion plan
Put your name in now if you can

Presentation visual perspective
Video of this project reflective
Harmon's full service store
Buy anything and more

DowntownRising.com
Learn where it's coming from
Rendering of City Creek appear
It will be completed some year

Lyrics of Light

Republican Precinct Chair Meeting

Republican precinct chair
Educated council there
How things work
Training not smirk

Introduction of officer care
James Evans is the chair
Helping a candidate
How can we relate

Quarterly with central body
Reports will not be shoddy
Approval of the budget
Fiscal year not fudge it

Know the procedure decision
What to decide not a division
Need to digest new information
Control data's help in creation

Not to happen: to do what I say
Really nothing will work that way
Talk on opposition NAACP
Not paying taxes, we see

12 Senate districts to chair
Elected next week to bear

Administer meet by email
Success to elect and sail

Difficult opposing entity
To communicate sympathy
Rick is vice-chair to work
Will help you and not shirk

Will not give one principle inch
Fighting opposition in the clinch
You are new and old
Seniors I am told

In charge of convention win
Do not spread it out too thin
Thank you for coming out
Together we have more clout

Financial statement
Robert Rice comment
Rick VC transparent
Questions are apparent

Get elected with exposure
1600 county delegates for sure
Caucus meeting feel
Will of body is for real

This is not very easy
Magnificently fuzzy
I am retired
Work not expired

Precinct is the basis core
Senate district 12 more
Legislative district is above
Work together as a glove

25 precincts per legislative
Work for all is suggestive
Duty of the of the chair
Knowledge of folks where

Basically central committee year
Learn and get in to gear
(This guy likes to talk
Makes you want to walk

Repetitive, cannot track
Talk about problem whack
We are the volunteers
Work is like the sheers

Casual in dress
And the address
Review to attend
Someone to send)

J. P. Hughes

We want you involved
Problems can be solved
Delegate to substitute
Another will constitute

We live for our by-laws
Our progress and the cause
Rational to make a change
Delegates can rearrange

Law is for control and order
Credentialed to enter at border
Windows is not always open
People verified and "hoppen"

Legislative District 24
Who I represent 2744
Convention will tick
New candidates pick

Republicans good to control
Nothing changes this roll
Process trumps the goal
Debris of interest is the toll

How we change the law
Support frustration's flaw
Fell through the crack
Centralized but lack

Lady from the back
PowerPoint lack
Complaint to see
Blame other, not me

Salt Lake County Clerk
Googled and it will work
Map of your precinct
Tell you what to think

Might reconsider and resign
Participate or refined
Be involved in the loop
Candidate votes to scoop

Bring five bucks
Pay for lucks
Send call by email
Not snail mail

We will not abuse
Something to use
We'll give it out
Party effort doubt

Randy O'Hara is resource
Walk on water, of course
Dana review blackberry
Officer's brain is hairy

County government structure
25 pages of by-laws
This is world of the delegate
1600 folks work to relegate

Review of the organization chart
We are here sitting and being apart
Nominating convention external
Organization of it all is internal

34 counties politically in this state
Committee is vibrant and will delegate
Robert's Rules of Order
Influence can order

I looked around
No familiar faces found
Used to know them all
No one now to call

It is so sad
Out of it bad
Do you get to know?
How these processes flow

Adult's behavior is poor
Getting smarter for sure
That was good use of time
Focus for best use is mine

Fund raising to measure
One half million treasure
Five hundred to attend
Politics of people send

Focus on the website
Review prevention's fight
791 precincts Republican vote
Determines formula for note

County party struggle
Objectives not haggle
Not off in weeds
Time wasted bleeds

Acrimony went away
Just be there and say
Not fight over things
Follow objective rings

If emotional out of order
The non-personal border
Not about humiliation
Work with conciliation

Keep emotion out
Ask, do not shout
All have a right
Or decorum blight

Burn up political capital
Not in charge of the chapel
We all make mistakes
Hopefully learn what it takes

We get hammered by the Press
Taking cheap shots will not suppress
May hear about rotten things
Controversial information brings

Beat me on my blog
My personality slog
May just disagree
But do not fight me

We are on the same side
We want work to glide
Three percent delegate futile
All day debate is brutal

Ability for a lesson
Free agent confession
Arm around the official
It is a good dismissal

What rules?
Broken fools
Cannot find it
Stir pot a bit

Wrap it up
Resource sup
How honest sample
Work in the temple

Whisper campaign
Involved the same
Do calling phone tree
Get ahold of me

Whole idea sits on hands
Then more passion fans
Pass out the information
Situation consternation

Get number of votes
Keep what floats
Voting records available
Chosen and capable

Sitting in chamber is sad
Names of who makes us mad
Not deep with emotion
Bored depth of commotion

One always in the room
Repetitive questions loom
It is universal
Always controversial

J. P. Hughes

Most are fat
Where they sat
All are white
Leaders in spite

Senate district chair
3 minute talk, but where
We can only endure
Idea to enjoy more

Have to work together
Distracted by one other
Recognized by the chair
Standing at the mic there

Robert Rules will speak
Say what you think
We want you there
Participation and care

Most interesting time
Keep on track to find
You are ready to go
This meeting to blow

Pornography Leadership

Inspired by an address from Monica Gardner

    We are at wit's end
    For a solution send
    You are familiar
    Are all similar?

    Sexual addiction
    Big time affliction
    Became a specialist
    Now like an evangelist

    No one wants an addict
    Give your skill for it
    Safety is first thing
    People depressed bring

    Child porno is a law
    Call hotline when saw
    No gray line
    It is not fine

    Is not just looking
    Masturbation hooking
    Not glossed over
    Keep filth's cover

Helps in weak moment
Recovery filter foment
Depression is a part
ECT even impart

Sensitive with emotion
Affects center's devotion
Women chat group
Is emotional poop

Word loser, freak
Self-thought leak
Self-esteem wide
Interaction abide

Untreated progression
Drug brain's obsession
It is a drug high
Repetitive sigh

Most try to repeat
Thinking it is neat
Gross stuff
It is not fluff

You get to love
Supportive above
Anger might dart
Emotion impart

Emotional autonomic
Compassion lack
Life-long not to tell
Not true as well

Some never do again
Stop struggle again begin
It is an emotional disorder
Shut down, overwhelmed odor

Look for congruity
Smirk, smile annuity
Not at time of remorse
Lying to you, of course

Some can cry and feel
For them it is a big deal
What do you want to be?
Help them answer and see

You are a coach
Then they will approach
They are accountable
You're encouraging surmountable

Condemning "no excuse"
They still return to abuse
Hurting other girls
Giving fantasy whirls

Objectifying a date
Outcome is too late
Narcissistic emotion
Life of lies commotion

No tenderness at first
Associations the worst
Back pocket arsenal
To use when we fall

Photos of family respect
Influence good aspect
Come up with own
Pictures to condone

Look at the happy place
Remember loving face
Best and brightest destroy
Evil's interest to employ

Internet is the tool
Of this generation fool
Triage of immorality
Time passing formality

Connection of confrontation
Admit to masturbation
They know the jargon
Part of dance's bargain

Calling, temple recommend
Denial's "yes" to commend
Difficult to handle
Really in the saddle

"Mess ups" just plain
Collective effort remain
Pandemic beyond border
Not a sexual disorder

Bailing out the boat
Keeping life afloat
Make me feel better
Work within the letter

Progress without finality
Just managing reality
No filter on the net
New home to bed wet

Protecting the computer
Not a control refuter
Watching porn
Watching adorn

Root is a feasting
Some not ceasing
Craze in darkness fight
Cure a principle of light

"Be the matter of man"
That you ought and can
Stop obsessing
Start confessing

The reward is porn
They just want more
Distractions of activity
Rewards over passivity

Conquering own Goliath
Feeling the dragon's breath
Need and help at night
To be strong and get it right

Feel good, not shame
Twelve Step program not blame
There are many others
Most of them your brothers

Leviticus talked about seed
Copulations on bed's need
Confronted of countenance
Cry easily at instance

How many times to quit?
Covenant with Lord a bit
"I am sick" everywhere
I do not want to be there

Lyrics of Light

Nothing gets in the way
"I will make it this entire day"
It is in way of my life
I will live to have a wife

You are perfect with Lord
Your hunger to change afford
Deceiving one another
Just running for cover

Call for help soon
Better than later swoon
Never give up
Never give up

A new life to earn
A time of concern
Your heart to learn
Character to discern

Salt Lake Community College

Listening to the team leader
As Foundation Board member
Hard to remember places
And the new faces

Wind out of sail
Introduction gale

Advisor, ambassador
Fundraiser for sure

Times of dysfunction
One about the unction
Working corporation
Planning the junction

Role planning
Advisors scanning
Vision's issues percolating
Answers quite stimulating

Responsible wisdom
Demonstrated for some
Ambassadorial role
Peers to control

Effective way
Share a model say
Grateful and considerate
Personally contribute

Remarkable to the world
Ambassador swirled
Love for the story to tell
Find out seed of the well

Simple in speech
Others to reach
Include in the talk
The leader to walk

Simple is the act
Health science fact
Significant comment
Happening content

Have you met to show?
Do you funding know?
Hosting in gathering
Graduation lathering

Look at area friends
To help SLCC ends
Cocktail camaraderie
Visit event menagerie

Need to be aggressive
Speaking to submissive
"Second fiddle" link
The way I used to think

But with a change
My mind's rearrange
Need to know a conduit
Recruit employee to suit

J. P. Hughes

Know about the event
Help and consent
Receive help now
Grass roots somehow

Get attention of affluence
And participating influence
Example of a student
Their lives and event

They provide a place
To give a smiling face
Recruit board members
Helping student remembers

High level of wealth
Working PAC stealth
All past political leverage
To learn others coverage

Seems like a simple way
Better the heart convey
Investor board and all
Gifts given do not stall

Transparency to see
Just giving from me
In a fundraiser
We work together

Difference of opinion
Plans for the reunion
Need major prospect
Priority and respect

Fund raising vision
Research in revision
Cultivate without division
Ask investor to envision

Then institutionalize
Process to rationalize
Capture to synthesize
Scholarship to conceptualize

Creation not criticize
Overlay to prioritize
Genetics to devise
Success to surprise

Location's listed
Campus insisted
Not just small
Colleges and wall

List what they know
Name where to show
Putting dollars to share
Accomplish goal where

Preliminary care urgency
In this campaign feasibility
Promotional now
Show them how

Access is the technical
Open door is the actual
Develop staff with fund
The work is never done

Nature of the calling
Is not that appalling
Build a file
Cultivate awhile

Ask and be a steward
Informed and assured
No fear of solicitation
Process demonstration

Gratitude in compensation
Strength in demonstration
Fun in the participation
Levels of excitation

Make a list
See who you missed
How do you go?
From a list to know

Focus on 3 to five
Major process revive
Reach out to those
That you suppose

Who will help you?
Not to worry or stew
"If you want money
Ask for their advice
If you want advice
Ask for money"

Learn about the answer
When "no" they swear
Why "no"
Money to blow

Committed to another
Issue with some other
It is a "bad day"
They might say

Options of interest
Spread out in nest
Estate planning option
Interest for adoption

Gain more
Start with sure

Reasons to contribute
What do you attribute?

What is the approach?
For this moving coach
Why do they give?
Admiration to live

Credit's recognition
Legacy's ambition
Good business sense
Family tradition's fence

Advocate direct mail
Honor process detail
Best in person to you
Find it in the value

Do your preparation
Important separation
Tell them why
Fundraising cry

Make request straight
Not entangling fate
Good idea heard
Gift not so absurd

On target modify
Listen to satisfy
Typically know money
Time is not funny

Listen, talk, and sell
Anticipate, not compel
Negotiate proposal
Take time to propel

"May I call" confess
Fundraising stress
Hard to fundraise
Their response appraise

Options to build
A program to shield
Multiple greeting
Not really competing

Compassionate resource
Bring others of course
Broaden the range
Typically arrange

Hit all the time
Good move to find
Need to know the deficit
Homework will benefit

Need the gift
Others to lift
Build momentum
To help others come

Ask outside the internal
Train, recruit the kernel
Written proposal
Passion disposal

Sincerity in segment
No cause to resent
Certain goal is the base
Target the segmental case

Field information size
Issue to institutionalize
Document the visit
"What did they say about it?"

Accountable strategy
Info base liturgy
Excel spreadsheet field
Thousands in file yield

Database marketing
Rich information
Pure consummation
Give a donation

Gain segmentation
What was old passion?
One-on-one impassion

Foundation's gift
Donation's lift
Pockets of prospects
Affliction's aspects

Possibility to identify
Then just ask why
Send thank you letter
Might feel a lot better

Please and thank you
Say what is true
Case study to overcome
Relationships: form some

Articulate interdependence
Pattern of giving confluence
Options of the field
What donor will yield?

Look at the possible
People not invisible
Overview of the mission
Take time about submission

Every citizen in valley
Affinity and value see
Symbolic literal presence
Summary is the essence

Rotary and the Tax

147 Years since Revenue Act
Income tax is the fact
10 years after war repeal
1913 the 16th amend to seal

1040 same as today
Work and then you pay
Stool with 3 legs faction
Thought, speech, and action

Act, interact, and be kind
Self, others, and God to find
Prayer means to focus
Thee in prayer the locus

Offering prayer every day
My plan to know what you say
Knowing self is not remote
Jews who live and devote

Life is to serve the one
Then another act is done

Of kindness and good
Doing what we should

Visitors at the Salt Palace
National convention finance
Joe Flynn Nelson retailers will see
Business, media, 9 billion in money

40,000 of 30 million to know
Excited for summer market show
Produced 11th year SLC to flow
Hopefully a lot of money blow

Media research advertising
Private trade show comprising
Construction big show
Attend shop to know

Sports group trade events
Different than leisure tents
Ski and the winter apparel
Sky stops shopping in peril

Eclectic stuff to mix
Inter bike Vegas fix
Largest 340,000 in space
Action in San Diego face

J. P. Hughes

Swim, sports, board, and ski
Exhibit in trade to see
Not a consumer show
By invitation to know

Stopped at the door
Big orders on floor
Buying power 30 billion
Industry difference a zillion

Dream of one
Put together in fun
Mark green surfer done
Grown up in industry run

Bike sales up
Gas coffee sup
Fast talker
Encouraging walker

Keep show here
Future business near
Ogden Canyon trial
Drew in consumer file

Winter market show
Associations know
Lobby in D.C. for open space
Keep in tract for next race

President Monson

He was an apostle at 36
In 1985 counselor to fix
ETB, HWH, GBH to now
The 16th President 2/3/08 how

Quieter of all
Young men tall
Challenges of a man
To learn of Spanish land

Assign him to Japanese
See if that will please
We are certain to learn
Creativity to earn

Funeral speaker
Getting through the beaker
Paid tribute to Brother Fife
Solace to mourning wife

Delivered it himself
Talent not on the shelf
Honor to be here
Uplifted to cheer

Grandma met on the sea
Determined what would be

Canadian mission president
Six months before J.P. was a resident

Liked Springer Spaniel
Pure bred not mongrel
Mother was Swede pure
Daddy Scott mongrel sure

What does it make you?
Mix of all not a few
Baptized in Tabernacle pool
Some in City Creek so cool

Two-and-a-half-minute talk
Prepare own and then to walk
On something that I like
Seagull monument tyke

Get coins from the water clear
Thrown away money far and near
Plowed plants for a cricket
Seagulls ate in the thicket

Talk to thirst
It was my first
What was the reply?
Baptism annulled the why

Get your sins restored
You're old and abhorred
Work hard not conspire
No lights out to inspire

Knew his flock
Ministered the block
Principles taught
Home teaching bought

Fulfill and duty learn
Collect Lord's to learn
Love origin of words
Stalk not absurd

What ought to be?
"As I am," you see
How to improve
Spirituality behoove

Have been at prayer
Now all aware
Theme to change
All bases rearrange

How did he type?
Report to swipe
All raised hand
Duty to perform in the land

Report of the stewardship
Have my deacon's quip
Do your duty all best
Leave the Lord the rest

Do you remember?
Inactive slumber
Party planned for best
Buy food 84 widows rest

Boys sang
Tears rang
Gifts to widow
Boys understood shadow

Blind to felt bench
Our heart to wrench
Go to each
A plant to reach

Little gift
Life to lift
Soda fountain
Fast Sunday maintain

Emblem of the ward
Envelope assured
Noticed shabby place
No food sorrow's face

Never revealed
No heavy hand sealed
Find a job
Never missed Bob

Best effort to help
Diligent in the difficult
Stalled one tough
His life so rough

Grabbed by shorts
Basketball arc retorts
Family revolved
Years later called

To bless
Questioned less
Spirit to go
Orange crate show

Book stand
Not remand
Fanned book
Alma 40 look

Now my son hurried
His mind worried
Spirits taken home
No longer roam

J. P. Hughes

But state of rest
The peace and best
He had the answer now
From Toronto somehow

Least likely to join in
Called by friend to begin
Seal my family remember
Here to be a new member

There was a crossing guard
Home teach from the Lord
Help children cross
Received not a loss

High Priest renegade
Not if lost to persuade
Teach and lead the way
Example yours to stay

Not a temptation
No suffering exportation
Just get out
If danger shout

Performance improves
Activity grooves
Individual or crowd
Coverage's shroud

Above the hinges
Or below that cringes
We want the people

Bishop, under the steeple
He was only twenty-two
With a thousand in the pew

Dark but came
Many remain
What advice?
Would suffice

Take care of the poor
Have no favorite sure
Feel no enmity
Search the divinity

Real poor to find
Found and remind
See if husband came
Helped building same

He was not there
Dear wife share
Strangest places
See their faces

J. P. Hughes

Be best all the same
All equal no click or blame
Essential for a move
Integrity to smooth

Make a bandage to cover
The wound that may hover
Would you read?
The manuscript's deed

Miracle of forgiveness
Will any be saved among us?
Try with a mighty thirst
With all your effort first

Many years ago
Forgive and show
Left tortured sin
In my office within

Will reduce strife
Come and love your wife
Women are better and aware
Happy home for us to share

Spirit will direct
Follow and select
The Lord knew
Our response to do

Instrument in word and call
My prayer is for all

Hinckley Institute

Inspired by an address given by Kirk C. Jowers

Candidate has things to do
Everyone wants to touch you
Obama or McCain
Longest ever campaign

No one would pick either
Voters may choose neither
19 primary candidates
Time snaps back in fate

Mitt Romney evident
First Mormon president
Attack to unite
Argument to invite

Primary and straw poll
Hard to tell or console
Primary about Hillary sure
Campaign interest to endure

Bill Clinton played it out
Her machine best no doubt

Obama revved up the internet
Greater power you may bet

Personal incredible gift
18–30 -year-olds to lift
Hinckley Institute
Voters resolute

Mixed member fate
Big swing too late
Obama preserver
Universal differ

McCain second in 2005
Coming out of the hive
Thought he would beat a few
Changed his organization new

George Allen shot his foot
Then blasted to the root
Giuliani not in top five
Republican not to revive

McCain is a maverick
Independent to stick
Republican in name only
Giuliani great fit but lonely

MMM Mormon Mass. Moderate
Huckabee not really considerate
Mitt led of the eight to defend
Disadvantage in the top ten

Name not known within
Looked like he might win
Romney to sew it up
Easily in primary cup

Huckabee found 30% hard
Played anti-Mormon card
Putin took Georgia in dust
Now McCain we can trust

He cannot raise money
Fired everyone not funny
Clinton continued the fight
Damage to Obama in spite

If he made it through
He could lead me and you
He got more registration
Reason for consternation

The vice-presidential pick
Could just make you sick
Interesting but conventional
Shown competent essentials

International event
"X" factor to relent
Negative attack
Interest lack

Numbers jumped a lick
When Palin VP he did pick
Not ready to become
An indictment for some

McCain's age is an issue
Might cry age with tissue
Obama keep sites
On the McCain fights

Candidate's win a stone
People appeal to moan
Obama polls way ahead
McCain campaign is dead

Volatility of polls to stick it
Ohio still a split ticket
Review by state
Polls too late

Large victory for Obama
Setting in now for drama
Narrow window without control
Keep going on this roll

Then question of the Senate
60 for the Democrats bent it
Uphill for them to know
If they'll control the show

Just get people to vote
Hold nose and connote
Negative if you lose
Facts and stories confuse

Undecided to find
Residents to remind
Run negative campaign
Vote for that to remain

One party left in power
Control it all this hour
People serving
Most deserving

Issues of state
People contemplate
Well run but improve
Wait and see to move

J. P. Hughes

To Fold Clothes

Inspired by Jana Allart. For twelve years, she ran a project called "the Exchange." On the second Saturday of every month, she would give away clothing donations she had collected.

Folding clothes
Given for those
Who in poverty chose
Warmth when wind the blows

A little giraffe toy
Stuffed for a little boy
Helping a little sister
Staring up at a mister

Quiet smile
Tender a while
Sacks filling
Weather chilling

Poverty's sad face
Of a giving embrace
Music and sound
People walking around

Tables of stuff
Consumers tough

Lyrics of Light

Some helping
Little kids yelping

Some sitting
Waiting or getting

Most of the time
My soul to remind
It's not about the clothes
It is the people who froze

It is about the process
It is about God to bless
It is the fun
It is seeing the Son

It is a smile of a child
It is a kid running wild
It is the question
It is the suggestion

It will make sense
If I am not so dense
It is not about the clothes
Tattoos, diversity, or a runny nose

Two little girls reading a book
Two women visiting to look

J. P. Hughes

One middle school boy
Helping pack a toy

One assigned to be here
Quiet not wishing to be near
"Want to be a geologist"
Helping recycled and missed

Some coming in late
Not much to debate
One sharing her pain
Shoulder surgery and drain

One grateful for a colonoscopy
Promised that it would be free
One who compliments
My example and intents

One giving a hug
One taking a mug
GED study need
For one trying to read

One to see and try
One taking as a magpie
One trying a fit
One in a chair to sit

Thank you, God
Hindu convert applaud
Helping to keep straight
Another planning a date

One getting baptized
After prison and smoking tried
One looking down
Or just glancing around

It is not about the clothes
It is not about the clothes

Bully

Bully prevention
Given attention
Always threatening
Worse by getting

What do we use?
When attitudes abuse
Safety is a right
Without a fight

Alternative skills
Proactive thrills
Research and treatment
Expectations of deferment

We need a prompt response
In the acquisition of defense
Progress is a treasure
Intervention to measure

Harassment's intimidation
Aggressive behavior station
Is repeating the negative
Exclusions of the inventive

There is cyber bulling
With others preying
The concept of the covert act
Starts with relationship's fact

Intentional and severe
Harassment to defer
Provocative peer
'Cliques' of popular near

If no supervision of the negative
Family become collaborative
Then starts absenteeism
With special needs chasm

If social deficit is exciting
Then an audience is inviting
We need to report the risk
Our response must be brisk

We need to create rules
Dealing with these fools
All need to be aware
Preventing 'the dare'

Impact learning
All of us concerning
Key of prevention
Is control's intervention

The next effective level
Of this problem to bevel
Is for all to enforce the skill
With support programs still

Core group and team
Assistance and beam
This is a bully blocker
Now cooperative stocker

Role play
Lesson stay
Talk and walk
Stalk and sock

Respect diversity
Not celebrate adversity
All should sign a pledge
On the bully ledge

"I agree
No bully from me.
I will include
If left out of the brood"

Sign your name
Never bully blame
Strategy to ignore
Thinking calm and sure

Goal setting
Bully getting
Not forgetting
Violence letting

Health Care Reform

Inspired by Amy Whettman

Health care reform
Presented in a storm
Market dynamic is local
Competition is focal

Strategic pricing
Icing and splicing
Managed care
Lost or aware

No one knows
Thinking shows
Key element
Coverage in cement

Focus on the well
Timing to tell
Quality outcome
Incentive for some

Medical record
Digital insured
Voice in development
Provide care with intent

Make money or loss
If toss away the cost
Lower the unit
Changes conduit

Bundled pay
All service way
Medicare impact
Accountable attack

Discharge plan
Reform we can
Providers and delivery
Data transparency

Consumer is aware
Their direction and care
Big ticket
Seminar to picket

Purchase model
Employee coddle
Ahead of the curve
Exchange or swerve

Compete with value
Loyalty stays with you
Compete by price
Better system splice

Critical preference
Will make the difference
Patients will look
In the quality book

Where is my Physician?
Satisfaction within
Marketing not bigger
Just find us better

Unit cost is critical
Outcome not theoretical
System integrated
Unique but debated

More alternate risk
Shared payer brisk
More information
Tight subjugation

Work with pay
Employ to stay
Bring value to gain
Olden times remain

Capitation delivery
The future will be
Guarded response
Incentive taunts

Imagine the rate
At Medicare debate
All patients pre admit
Or a penalty submit

Be aware of the care
Of our ideas to share

Our Experiment

Ninety percent did not vote
In the Primary election to note
"My vote does not count" it is fine
My vote never cast was hard to find

In the General election to defend
Eighty percent did not vote again
If two years later and now
Two thirds will not vote somehow

It must be said
Democracy is dead
It will never survive
Left to others to connive

It was a great experiment
For me I will lament
To live free to be
To be what I can see

I know where it is going
Where Democracy is flowing
To the end
Not to mend

To an abyss
Democracy I will miss
Participate, Activate, Dedicate
Consecrate, Illuminate, Educate

Medicine

A Letter

In my business letter
Would it not be better
To write it short
A note to report?

"I saw your patient"
Who is now content
I did my best
In treatment's quest

Of the endoscopic test
Now you can rest

Innovation

This will be my last time
Salt Lake Surgical wine and dine
Laughter, guffaws loud
Where you sitting in this crowd

People new and talk
Around table they will walk
No idea about the seating
No courtesy or any greeting

I am a vascular surgeon
Peter Schneider to begin
Teaching four kids bike to ride
Not getting anywhere with pride

Bike technology is risk-taking bid
Keep an eye on this kid
Dad does not know what he is doing
You taught me in no time, no fooling

Disruptive technology tolerate
Disrupts the status quo, appreciate
People to innovate and knock
To open a can with chisel and rock

Side effects of the digital phone
Make land line owner moan

J. P. Hughes

From something that did not exist
Now to something we cannot resist

Anthropology is a boring read
Explain how culture work and bleed
Climate, agriculture, and food
Winter and political correct mood

Every complex problem has simple solution
It is always wrong as is pollution
Laparoscopic replaced me right
I was obsolete over night

England lags all others
Not innovative brothers
Ready to ride or not
Galen 1708 trochar sought

Product, service, method change
Unexpected status quo re arrange
Keyhole surgery fool
Laser and you are cool

The car, digital photo done
Semiconductor and the sun
Endovascular technique
Magna Charta 1215 oblique

First time monarch had no power
Absolute no longer as of this hour
Revised over 500 years
Refinement low-end market tears

Toyota Corolla going low-end
Others to drive we will send
Lack of refinement
Least demanding confinement

Sustaining technology as stable
Improving performance if able
Established products to change
If not, out of range

Reality TV with Survivor
Disruptive then reviver
Aneurysm, open triple A
Big operation to survive this way

Triple A stent graft
No large operating staff
Total number increased
Seven times higher pleased

Mortality rumored much less
Customer insight confessed
Innovators mad scientist alone
Not done by committee condone

Loners that do not get along
Eloquence of complexity' song
Innovators safe environment hear
Compliance regulation nowhere near

The secret of creativity is to know
How to hide your source or show
Where does the source come from?
Spiritual, intellectual, emotions, palm

Captain Cook first European in travel
Greenwich museum ships and naval
Power was present and most aware
Disruptive exploration not very fair

Most would chart a course
Never return three-fourths remorse
Chronometer helped go and return
Cape Horn discovery to learn

Success to go and come back
Was sauerkraut, vitamin C no lack
Prevented scurvy and the song
De Galma lost most of crew belong

Bad ideas from boardroom talk
Logical decisions increment walk
Improvement did not work for the SUV
Stupidity on the road for all to see

Lyrics of Light

Power of context referral
Was not spending on the rural
This is how it was
Follow orders just because

Training is exhausting on site
Emphasis on "do it right"
This way done every time a clue
Not best to innovate anything new

Body snatcher origin past
We are at risk at last
Not free market to control
Protectionism of standard roll

Price control does not work
Will not do anything but shirk
Randomized trial a quirk
Failure system here to lurk

Innovation will get cocky alone
We become our own technology bone
Gastroenterologist smartest doc
Became a technological lock

Endoscope above or below
Contribution of both they know
Innovator creates something for need
Does not make sense to those who lead

The innovator is complex in nuance
The work like the Renaissance
His new idea may appear crazy
But he works it out and is not lazy

The early adopter makes it go
More often separate you know
The story is simply told
Enthused about it and bold

These are the tweakers
And opportunity seekers
It is all about the money
And to them it is not funny

The connectors light the brush fire
They seed the world and inspire
The late adopters are not status quo
They can make millions and know

It cannot be done any way
Should be done ethically they say
I can do it better than good
We can change a little and would

Ovarian Cancer

CT scan ovarian Ca mesenteric caking
In peritoneum cancer baking

Ovarian carcinoma abhor
Worse carcinomatosis for sure

Ascities and everything struck
Pelvis foreseen resection no luck
Debulking colon, spleen, ovary all
Suffering vena cava filter DVT call

Poorly differentiated papillary serous
Gall bladder wall tumor there near us
Myometrial wall invaded everywhere
Surface and ascities T3CN staged care

Surgeon explaining survival
Statistic and debulking revival
Thirteen months extended at 70 years
Recovery time neo adjuvant appears

Advocate in fighting ring
Surgeon extensive diaphragm bring
Non-resective around aorta mets
Would not do it rule but lets

Surgery time sounds of 9 hours
Randomized trials cowers
Aggressive debulking evidence
Long answer significant cycle dance

J. P. Hughes

Millions of cells diminished respond
Have to give chemo way too long
Trials open clinical talk
Game study participation walk

Avastin, carboplatnum and pain
Surface primary peritoneal serosal remain
The spread of cancer is everywhere
Surgically attack, if you dare.

Cancer

Perineal lesion in the midline
Bloody mucus discharges not find
Muscinous adenocarcinoma treat
Radiation to kill, tumor beat

Re-excisional biopsy in the crease
DVT, PE, myopathy asthma and obese
Local recurrence radical excision call
Close and hopefully free of rectal wall

One half mm margin to close
Lower and higher margin suppose
Squamous metaplasia cell
Skin origin happens to tell

Diagram white board art
Wide excision tumor to depart

What to do from here
For small margin near

Stay Here

I think I will stay
I feel it deep some way
I might have to give a talk
Conference session thought to lock

A 23-week pregnant patient call
An abscess is back, twins and all
She lives in Pleasant Grove
I am glad I stayed, not drove

They met me at six
I drained abscess to fix
When they left tear in my eye
I saved a suffering life reply

Then typed 14 pages of anon
This poetry-creating demon
Met M.D. on walk at home
Visited our house to roam

He volunteers for orphans
In Peru with medical demands
Going to Africa soon
OB-GYN knowledge a boon

Gave him a ticket to conference session
Maybe that is why to stay confession
He came to comfort sister with twins
21 weeks and in hospital until it ends

The highlight of the decision
Was with Jessie Rhodes revision
Meeting him with his father
From Wisconsin no bother

Salt Lake Surgical

Inspired by an address from Dr. Peggy Knudsen

Trauma from war
Learned here afar
Iraq teaching care
Battalion aware

Evacuation ambulance
Medical help stance
Military IED injuries
Repair, shunt, fixator sees

All about transport
To get support
Trained all consort
Improvement report

Combat use of blood
Stay, stabilize crud
Evacuated to Germany
Stay and re-explore any

All assume contaminated
Arrival transfer illuminated
Compartment changes abscess
Stabilized incredible process

System tied together
Treatment weathered
Many traumas MD's time
Be there and hear the rhyme

Help the rotation
Allow flotation
Not real silence
Medical reliance

Landstuhl hospital renter
Now the medical center
Busy arrive in bus
Staffed by us

All work together
Army, Navy another
Op note resection and stoma
What was done at trauma?

Each MD takes a patient sight
Work for twelve hour flight
Amazing on this focus
Scheduled MD night for us

Grateful for midnight
Time to do it right
Burns, blast penetrating
Explosive fragment concentrating

Frag jar injury device
Found in patient suffice
Burns from melted humvee
Worse thing you could see

MDs came to help stabilize
Goal to get out conceptualize
SNEED with ventilator
On top of patient sent here

Scary part of the journey
Flight with patient on gurney
Assorted medics revere
Intubated patient most severe

Physical exam in the air
Pulmonary embolus where
Andrews or San Antonio
Unload and not solo

Vent, chest tube, and Foley
Developed critical slowly
Air fuel tanker revise
Fitted for care surmise

Iraq with military pace
Protection in this place
Red-tail fliers separate
African pilots commiserate

Conference held in Iraq
Earmarked trailer smack
Had to have Kevlar
Siren blown in war

Building not a tent
Prepare for rocket sent
Helicopter brings them in
Ambulance only base begin

Category of causality taught
Children often shot
CT scanners all right there
Helping in short time where

No one yelling but could
Working hard and should
Civilian medical care
Devastated everywhere

Live hot wire sad
Amputated with no rehab
No infrastructure
Bad boys conjecture

Interesting patch for wall
That is not all
Trauma, died of wound
Lowest death rate boon

Learned and take to heart
Tourniquet all a part
Seen deployed for a bleed
Tourniquet if you need

Ultrasound used
Surgeons not abused
Now hemopheumo thorax
Echo cardiogram to ask

Damage control for resuscitation
Hypotensive blood replaced in station
Factor VII a given first
Stop bleeding burst

TED monitor thanks
Walking blood banks
Control pressure and save
Shunts not heparin brave

Healthy men with muscle brave
Compartment fasciotomy save
Contamination control
Colon injury stoma mole

First sent VAC
London to Iraq
Put it on braved
Wounded saved

Pulitzer Prize with child
TBI wound head wild
PTSD high problem aware
Several patients in burn care

Silver dressing for seven days
Staple on wound, it stays
Quick clot and tourniquet
Designed truck protect

The system is competent
Database information supplant
JPTA trauma show
Save patient you know

VTC video trauma conference
Online hear voice and stance
Wonder and speak immediate
Note at history expedient

End is Polytrauma Center aware
Medical for lost eye, arm and care
IED vascular brain
Lost mush to drain

Stay in small place
Driving simulator face
Prosthetic replaced to see
Computer placed in knee

Amazing to be a part
Psychotherapy to impart
Retrial about a girl
Prostheses give a whirl

Bilateral amputee
With computerized knee
Traumatic limb
Fins to swim

New look
Leg forsook
Feel it in toes
Realized, knows

Was on TV
Want you to see
Believe in war
Hope and progress sure

Iraq is awful place stressing
Every breath is depressing
IPOD with Anderson Cooper
He is informational TV super

American Cancer Society

American society
Survival variety
Gain friendship
Their mentorship

Support from love
Affected people a dove
Unforgettable example
Strength of life's sample

Help family and friends
Cancer survival never ends
Mother and wife had cancer
Fine, now progress's anchor

Service support resource
Information given of course
Patient navigator process
Professional service recess

IMC has a center and some
There is the helping of the one

Volunteer of this society gears
Service and help over the years

Core program fund
Help financial some
Not off the hook
Going to class to look

This is a clock
Recipient flock
Hard to knock
Service never balk

Two-year-old treated sane
Wilm's tumor in Hurricane
With 30 also from 12 years old
Amazing stories were told

Nutrition campaign
Program activity complain
Health and wellness
Common sense and fitness

Screening and activity
Give hope to longevity
Recipient of this gift
Feelings of life to lift

Historic decline
Research remind
Thank you fund
Donor gift some

Basic cell divide
Argue cancer reside
Abnormal cell division
Terrible result revision

Faithfully divide cell
Coordinate this well
Study one gene
Around nucleus seam

Dispersing to slow
Cancer not to grow
Target cancer cell
Thank for research bell

Impact of research
As we progress and lurch
Nobel Prize at the end
Recognize and send

Recipient study of damage
Failure of cell to rummage
Cell Drosophila's telomere
Damage and mutation sure

Will cell still divide?
Key to cancer reside
Mechanism to grow
New gene to know

How does it start?
Cell coming apart
Award of scholar
Result from dollar

Survivor like a lance
Children in living stance
Work and endure
Obstacle for sure

Pursue with scholarship fund
Contribute, receive, and run
Vernal relay race and dollar
Successful for us to holler.

It makes you cry
As you ask why?
Suffering with pain
What do we gain?

Youth walk to stage
Deep cell division rage
They came and stood
Received help and should

Make this disease of pain
Memory not to remain
All invited to stand
Each a cure we can

Dad quiet and in tears
Daughter happy, it appears
14-year-old tumor in brain
Headaches, nausea drain

Seeing double
There must be trouble
Pressure on optic nerve
CT changes curve

Size of tumor then hair
Surgery went well there
Two years later again
Hats to wear and thin

Radiation next step
Received accepted crept
Body not right
Too many dates blight

Seizure then MRI
Diagnosis third tumor, why
Supposed to cry later
Angry with God and Seder

One thing that I learned
Not more than I can handle earned
Learned about faith, prayer, and hope
The fight goes on with spiritual soap

I studied in London about art
Huge bills to pay and part
Wonderful to help student
Time from us to rent

Not a dry eye snapped
All stood and clapped
Extraordinary visionary
Pioneer and illuminating

Read about my friend
Many projects send
Registrar to know
Volunteers to show

Remarks and comment
Daughter's amazing torment
Will make a difference won
I am emotionally undone

They have gone to battle more
Dr. Smart was an early warrior
Punching data entry level
Research change to revel

It affected these kids
Cancer knowledge rids
What we should do
Coffin viewing blue

It is malignant see
Fight ahead for me
Sword of Hope Award
1992 received accord

Research doctor, giver
Drastic change to deliver
There is the Smart way
And then the intelligent way

He was passionate about this
Raise our sword tighter, miss
IMC Hospital to receive
Cancer suffering to relieve

Received with respect
Research to suspect
Learn, listen, and hear
The cure is so near

Focus effort true
Produce results anew
Wake up with a dream
Brighter night will seem

IMC Surgery Department

Inspired by an address given by Mark Ott

Life healing
Profession sealing
Economy recession
Political confession

Small visiting talk
Every experience walk
Hospital character able
Interpreting the variable

Expected complication
Statistical variation
Sampling of cases
Determine the bases

Collection of information
Learning supplication
Mortality on a graft
Ratio level not a laugh

Morbidity statistic
Improvement ballistic
Change by viewing
Impact by renewing

Lyrics of Light

Use of Beta blockers
Thinking not lockers
Continuing Attenalol
Confusion and all

Ownership of info
Pneumonia to show
Head of bed
Elevated instead

Repeating the reiteration
Tease out and requisition
Hours on ventilator
Comparison revelator

DVT rate screen and date
Risk electronic fate
Searching sentry
STDs on risk entry

Heparin Lovenox repeating
Trade off operative bleeding
Complication's conceding
Death defeating

Outliers value space
Check off a new face
Orders by default
PIC line assault

Patients in renal failure
Post-op drugs for sure
Education one-on-one
Lividity if another done

UTI cath and culture
In place as a vulture
Every patient called
Red drainage appalled

Mortality and morbidity
Patient in liquidity
How can we improve?
Our behavior behoove

Decisions

How do you know?
Where you should go
When to apply?
Or should you try?

It may not be logical
Or could be mythological
It is always inconvenient
But may be expedient

Will it ensure?
My future endure

Will it make a change?
That I can rearrange

Is it a win-win?
Scheduling when to begin
Will there be a choice?
Will they listen to my voice?

Can I adapt then?
Can I start when?
What will I do?
Experience and teaching you

I love to teach
Others to reach
This is my chance
For veteran's branch

To have hospital privileges
Medical affairs and new bridges

Foreign Bodies

Foreign body removal
In emergency upheaval
Becoming medical challenges
Of the index finger phalanges

J. P. Hughes

Glass test tube or irrigation bulb
Billiard ball or dildo's flub
The TV remote is lost
Removal increases the cost

Vegetable of phallic size
Insertion lost to surprise
Wire stirring handle whisk
Removal cannot be brisk

They always wait to see
If they can pass it out and be
Relieved of the pain
Without success they strain

The situation is embarrassing
As the patient is undressing
The origin of the story
Could be kind of gory

The doubting stare
Or kindness aware
I can remove these
With patience, please

On the patient's left side
Or in pelvic stirrups wide
Sedation will relax
Making removal a fact

Left hand suprapubic shift
Right hand digitally lift
Ask the patient then to strain
The foreign body will not remain

Place a Foley catheter inside
If a hollow foreign body resides
Blow up the balloon
Removal will be soon

With a tug, push, and shout
It will come sliding out
Flexible endoscopy to see
Where a tenaculum could be

Placed on the foreign end
Pulled carefully to send
Kindness with a smile
Will remain a long while

ACLS

Inspired by Linda Edwards

BLS changed
ACLS rearranged
There is a new video update
New material to contemplate

Standards are new
Card holders few
"Everyone will pass"
Taking this class

Hands that sweat
Examinations forget
Consequences high
Pass or die

Synopsis of disease
Cardiovascular please
Advanced Cardiovascular Life Support
ABCD to chest compression report

Check response to live
Activate system to give
Carotid pulse to see
Successful use of the AED

Chest compression first
Even if ribs are to burst
100-per-minute compress
High quality, hard and fast
Push deep if you can last

Two inches deep fact
Allow time to retract

From this heart attack
Switch roles, energy lack

Compression is the goal
Brain loss is the toll
Quickly check the pulse
Ten seconds impulse

Defibrillation
Without hesitation
Check, then activate
Pulse to contemplate

Change in algorithm there
After cardiac arrest care
Identify the cause aware
Hypothermia therapy stare

Comatose called to see
What the circumstance will be
How long has he been down
Before he was found on the ground?

With STEMI or PCA
Cath lab is where to stay
Airway change
Capnography strange

Confirm the placement
CO_2 waveform sent
No cricoid pressure
Agonal breath treasure

Chain of survival
Delivery of arrival
Twelve lead EKG
Advance time to see

Stroke time is brain
Alert hospital in time
Survival specialize
Fibrinolysis comprise

IV, history exam
X-ray and demand
O_2, ASA, NTG, morphine
For a better result seen

ST segment depression
Door to balloon impression
Rapid response team
Serious situation gleam

Bradycardia relative or absolute
Simplified to contemplate
The course and the team
Are life and death, it would seem

Addiction

Addiction as an affliction
Addiction with infliction
Treatment like infection
Etiology and prediction

Why not get an MRI
To diagnose and try
Magnetic Resonance Image
Lights up in brain's foliage

Maybe it is like a seizure
To surgically needle the fissure
And with a probe and place
Destroy the synapse in this space

Then there would be a cure
The afflicted now more sure
To live a life of peace
With the demons that cease

Health Department Grant

Colon cancer screening
Work plan beaming
Comprehensively can
Letters of support demand

Data in a draft
Community craft
Detail to commit
Little to remit

Lost referral
Liability swirl
Narrative clean
CDC grant seem

Contract number
Officially slumber
Make understanding
Specifically demanding

Partners on board
Agreement assured
Problems are legal
Lawyer as a beagle

Health insight so far
Or a mountain star
Who to contact
Communicate intact

Utah cancer specialist
Who will help on a list?
Listening on the phone
Maybe inattention prone

It is a media thing
Grant writing brings
Need data analyst
Share priority insist

More efficient eyes
Incorporated complies
When the calls came in
Their sincerity spin

Was the time to see?
What this could be
To help the uninsured
Have help assured

It was the feeling
Of careful dealing
With so many
Who cannot get any?

Of the screening exam
In a society of man
Who we need to support
And then turn in the report

J. Preston Hughes was born in 1942 in Spanish Fork, Utah. He served a Latter-day Saint mission to Quebec and Ontario, in the Eastern Canadian Mission. He received his BS in zoology from Brigham Young University and his MD from the University of Utah. He is married to Elaine Jones and together they have six children and seventeen grandchildren.